Take a SHOWER, show up on TIME, and don't STEAL anything!

& OTHER SH*T I LEARNED THE HARD WAY

by DAVE RYAN

This is a work of creative nonfiction. The events are portrayed to the
best of Dave Ryan's memory. While all the stories in this book are true,
some names and identifying details have been changed to protect the
privacy of the people involved.

ISBN 13: 978-1-940014-58-6
eISBN: 978-1-63489-000-7

Library of Congress Catalog Number: 2015935682
Printed in the United States of America
First Printing: 2015

19 18 17 16 15   5 4 3 2

Cover design by Kevin Cannon
Interior design and typesetting by Ryan Scheife / Mayfly Design
and typeset in the Chaparral Pro and Curse Casual typefaces

Wise Ink Creative Publishing
Minneapolis, MN
www.wiseinkpub.com

To order, visit www.itascabooks.com or call 1-800-901-3480.
Reseller discounts available.

CONTENTS

Introduction 1

1. Take a Shower 5

2. Show Up On Time 51

3. Don't Steal Anything 91

Conclusion 135

Acknowledgments 137

About the Author 138

"Good judgment comes from experience, and a lot of that comes from bad judgment."

—WILL ROGERS

INTRODUCTION

I made my first real mistake when I was four years old. I'd made mistakes before then, I'm sure, but this one was a monster.

My mom was on the upstairs phone, talking to our neighbor. I, being four, wanted attention. So I did the one and only thing I knew would get her to focus on ME.

I went downstairs, picked up the other phone, and said the most powerful word I could create: *shit-ass*.

Coming out of anyone, that's a serious attention grabber; it's somewhat uncommon, it sparks the imagination, and best of all, it's two swear words in one. Coming from the mouth of a four-year-old, it succeeded in getting me the attention I wanted . . . and more.

The next few minutes were a blur of yelling, spanking, hair pulling, and labor strikes, and I'm pretty sure an arson fire was even set nearby. I quickly learned from my mistake of using *shit-ass* in mixed company.

I'd have to save it for when I was hanging with my siblings who thought it was hysterical when I said it.

Like you, I've made plenty of mistakes in my life.

I've said the wrong thing at the wrong time to the wrong person, taken the wrong job, picked the wrong person to fall in love with, and used the wrong fork at a fancy restaurant.

Consequences can be large or small, but either way, mistakes can be embarrassing, like the time I mistakenly called a hiring manager "Biff" instead of his actual name (Bill) during a daylong job interview. Mistakes can be expensive. I trusted someone who promised if I invested in a rat-trap office building in Tampa, I'd get a huge return on my investment. I lost all of it. Mistakes can be painful. I fell so hard learning to snowboard that it made me sick to my stomach. The bruise on my butt was the size of a pumpkin.

Still, mistakes are one of the best teachers in the world. I've been bitten by every Chihuahua I ever tried to be friendly to, so I learned that I just don't mix well with these adorable yet ferocious little creatures.

There are people who make the same mistakes over and over again. Maybe they date a loser who steals their mom's jewelry and can't stay out of jail. How miserable. You'd think that one bad experience would be the last. But nope, people will get rid of one loser boyfriend only to hook up with a felon who smokes the wicker futon and can't pay his child support. Or how about the guy who got fired for stealing toilet paper from work last year *and*

2

last week!? I mean, I get it to a degree. We all screw up, but most of us, if tased by a cop for taking a wild swing at him, will think twice before we do it again. Trust me, I've also made the same mistakes, BIG mistakes, more than once before I learned my lesson.

Paraphrasing self-help guru Anthony Robbins, "Learning from experience is really effective, it's just time consuming!" This book is jam-packed with 101 of the most common (or common sense) life mistakes that I've made myself OR that I see others making. But this book isn't just about mistakes; it's a book about how not to be an asshat. It's a book about how to benefit yourself and the rest of the human race by following simple, practical advice. And following this advice will benefit you not just now, but in your reputation going forward. If I can convince my son not to be a thief, it'll save him the trouble of being blamed every time a pencil goes missing at his future job. If I can convince my daughter not to get a giant neck tattoo, I can save her the trouble of being turned down for any job that earns more than minimum wage. I know it all sounds judgmental, but here's a new flash: our society IS judgmental—they just pretend they're not. I want to help you be judged for how awesome you are, not for your impressive shoplifting skills.

It all starts with the basics. After I learned not to blurt out "shit-ass" in mixed company, I learned to avoid other mistakes, like not bathing, showing up late, and being busted stealing a plunger from the men's room at work. (When you need a plunger, *you need a plunger*!)

Making habits from those three simple rules—I call them my "Big Three"—is a great place to start! And yes, I know YOU already know to take a shower, show up on time, and not steal anything, but could you *possibly* name someone you know who struggles with these ideas? Yeah, me too.

I'm not pulling punches in this book, and I'll likely offend some people on one topic or another. When I say a thirteen-year-old kid shouldn't have blue hair and your kid does, you might not like that very much. You might say, "It's just hair! She doesn't want to be like everyone else!" as teachers and neighbors snicker at you and mutter funny things about your parenting style. I'd say if she doesn't want to be like everyone else, how about she picks up the oboe? NO ONE plays the freakin' oboe anymore. But wait, that would be too hard. Yep, dying her hair blue is definitely the better answer.

I have a feeling, though, that between periodic grumblings of what a judgmental jerk I am, you'll be nodding your head in agreement with most of what you'll read in this book. After all, you had the good sense (not to mention the few extra dollars) to buy it. Unless you stole the money out of your girlfriend's mother's purse, in which case, you and I are going to have a problem.

Part 1

Take a
SHOWER

This sounds super basic, doesn't it? You and I learned in elementary school that the smelly kid gets shunned. If he still smells by the time middle school rolls around, then this poor kid is destined for more than his share of ridicule. There are plenty of adults who smell awful, too. You've sat next to one on the plane, stood behind one at the DMV, and you probably even have one at your office. I don't get it. Do they not realize they smell like a combination of wet dog and a Porta-John? Do they actually think no one will notice it's been days since they showered? Maybe they don't notice their own bad smell because they *always* smell!

I've had to tell a few people who worked on my radio show to take a shower and wear clean clothes each day. Not only did I feel awful doing that, but it was also über-humiliating for them. One was an intern who never came into work again. It's too bad, but someone had to tell him. I took one for the team and let him know because everyone else who worked with him was tired of him coming to work smelling like a rodeo.

Someone who smells like a rodeo isn't going to get promoted. Not ever.

#2 OVERDRESSED IS ALWAYS BETTER THAN UNDERDRESSED

It was time to attend one of my first office Christmas parties, so I put on a new sweater and a pair of nice pants. When I walked in and saw all the other guys in suits and ties, I knew I'd blown it. My date and I both felt pretty stupid the whole night, even though no one said anything.

Fast forward to last summer's grand opening of a rooftop restaurant in downtown Minneapolis. Me? (I'm not in my early twenties anymore.) I'm decked out in my Old Navy cargo shorts and a Polo shirt. This time, someone did say something. My boss spotted me, walked up, gave me a warm handshake, and said with clenched teeth and a smile, "You're underdressed."

Guess what I've learned? It's always better to be overdressed than underdressed. Imagine you're in Caribou Coffee and someone walks in dressed like they just stepped off a modeling runway in New York. Do you snicker and say, "Look at that overdressed idiot..."? No.

Chances are, you figure they're either very important or just plain fashionable. Wear cargo shorts to a nice restaurant and people will notice ... just not in a good way.

#3 HAVE A CLUE ABOUT POLITICS

Politicians tend to be attractive for a reason. People who haven't been paying attention usually vote for the more attractive candidate. Or worse yet, they vote for the candidate endorsed by their favorite celebrity. Honestly, I don't know how an ugly candidate who isn't endorsed by Adam Levine could ever get elected. Thank God they occasionally do, which proves there *are* people who pay attention.

Politics can be boring, especially when you're young. It takes some effort to find out what is really going on, and besides, it is way easier to just let someone else worry about it. The problem is, politics are *actually* kind of important. History shows us that countries can crumble because of bad politics and bad government. Maybe you've heard of the USSR or that guy Hitler? Sitting around trusting politicians to do the right thing is kind of like that weekend your mom and dad trusted you to watch the house while they were gone. You assured them you'd be doing homework all weekend and going to bed early each night, but while they were in Vegas, blissfully unaware, you had forty friends over who got drunk, peed in the dishwasher, and smashed your mom's Precious Moments collection.

A friend of mine told me she was voting for a popular candidate because "She'd make a good president." When I asked her what made this candidate so right for the job, she had no idea and took the opportunity to bash me for gettin' all up in her business. People hate it when you point out how dumb they seem.

It's your money, your community, your state, and your country. If the only thing you know about politics

---

People hate it when you point out how dumb they seem.

---

is that weed should be legalized and that every American deserves a sweet sixty-five-inch flat screen, you might be a little behind the curve. Pick up a magazine (or download one), read some blogs, or ask someone you respect. If that fails, just ask me, and I'll tell you exactly what you should think.

#4 LITTERING—REALLY?

Littering is one of those things that confounds me. Who would decide it's okay to toss an empty Dairy Queen cup out the car window? Yet, it's obvious just by looking on the ground that there are people who do it just as casually as they turn without signaling or cough without covering their mouth.

I was in the heart of downtown Minneapolis when I saw two guys in their twenties walking on the sidewalk of a busy street. Without even a moment's hesitation or effort to find a trashcan, one of the guys tossed his empty Monster Energy drink can on the sidewalk. As it clanked down into the gutter, I opened my mouth to say something and then quickly realized that someone clueless enough to do that would probably have no problem shanking me, so I kept my mouth shut.

To take it a step further, I teach my kids to pick up litter when they see it. If we're at the park and someone has thrown an empty Pringles can on the ground, we pick it up and throw it away. Sure, it's not our trash, but let's face it—we already spend a lot of time doing things for people who should be doing things for themselves, so what's a few more seconds?

#5 MOST OLD PEOPLE WERE YOUNG ONCE

I was at a pancake breakfast and a couple came in who had to be in their eighties. They kept to themselves and ate quietly. I started up a conversation by asking, "Are you from around here?" Turns out, they'd lived in town for fifty-seven years and told me all about how the town had changed over time. All they needed was someone to ask them about it.

Same pancake breakfast, the guy serving sausage was at least eighty as well. Once I got him talking, I found out that his great grandparents moved to town in 1853 and had great memories of how they used to get along so well with the Native Americans in the area. They even have a park in town named after them!

We often forget that old people used to be young. We fail to realize that they don't talk about bursitis and share vivid descriptions of their bowel patterns. Nope, they actually have a wealth of things to talk about, if only we take the time to ask.

Not only was it fascinating to hear these stories, I came away feeling like I made their day a little brighter by showing some genuine interest in them. Talk to old people. They won't be around much longer to tell you their story.

#6 THANK YOUR PARENTS

Appreciate your parents. They're not around as long as you wish they would be.

My mom and I were pretty close when I was growing up. By "pretty close," I mean I was a complete mama's boy. She spoiled me rotten and I considered her one of my best friends, right behind my cigarette-and-booze-providing buddy, Scott.

My dad and I weren't close when I was a kid, mostly because he was the old-fashioned and strict sort of parent and I was a little asshole. I can count on one hand the number of times he spanked me, but if he'd done it once a day, I tell you today I would have deserved it. Dad was my Boy Scout leader, taught me how to shoot a gun, and made me help butcher chickens every Fourth of July when all the other Americans were splashing around in a lake and having a picnic.

Growing up with a dad who made me work was a giant pain in the ass and I completely hated it. I spent countless hours avoiding my dad by playing Kiss records in my room, hoping he wouldn't come find me. I swear I could hear the sound of his cowboy boots approaching my room, even over the sound of "Detroit Rock City." The door would open without a knock, my cue to "turn that noise down." He would say, "I've got a whole lot of wood on the hill for you to cut up." My dad didn't mean I could do it sometime next week or after I was done watching *The Dukes of Hazzard*. He meant NOW. I suppose he'd allowed some time for me to put some shoes on and maybe hit the bathroom first, but other than that, he meant NOW. I swear he'd come up with meaningless work just so I wouldn't get in the habit of sitting around too much. If he found me watching television, he'd send me out to the hill behind our house to pick up sticks to use as kindling for the fireplace. This was a totally unnecessary job because we already had a seven-story stack of kindling. If I wanted to go fishing with my buddies, he made me do some mundane chore first. "Sure, you can go, but there's a whole garden that needs weeding first," he would say.

When I was twenty years old, I moved to my own apartment and it was bliss. No more wood-splitting, chicken-plucking, or weed-pulling Saturdays for me! No more answering to the old man. I remember he was a little sad when I put my last load of stuff into my car and told him goodbye, but I didn't care. I was FREE!

Over the next twenty years, I noticed something. A lot of people are lazy. They do just enough work to keep them from getting fired. The whole work ethic thing that Dad taught me started to pay off. While a lot of my co-workers muttered things like, "They don't pay me enough to do that," or "That's not my job," people came to me to get things done because they knew I'd probably do it. Not only that, but I was pretty likely to do it right the first time.

A lot of people are lazy.

Mark Twain once said, "When I was a boy of fourteen, my father was so ignorant I could hardly stand to have the old man around. But when I got to be twenty-one, I was astonished at how much the old man had learned in seven years."

It's the same with my dad and me. All the work and responsibility that I hated as a kid prepared me to succeed in life.

Before I got a chance to thank my mom for spoiling me rotten, she slowly got dementia, and by the time I realized I wanted to thank her, she barely knew who I was. I hope somehow she knew how much I loved her and appreciated all she'd done for me. About a month before my dad died, I thanked him for all the things he taught me and for all the time he spent with me when I was a kid. Dad was a man of few words. "You're welcome" was all I got out of him, but that was enough. I'm glad I got to say it.

#7 IF YOU CAN'T AFFORD TO EAT OUT, THEN DON'T

Don't bring packets of Crystal Light to the restaurant and then order "just a glass of water." If you can't afford a Diet Pepsi, then you can't afford to eat out. It's the same thing with tipping. No one is working as a server because that's their dream career. Nope, they do it so they can

afford groceries and the latest cellular technology. Help 'em out with a generous tip. If you can't afford to buy a drink or tip your server, you can stay home and fix yourself some microwave popcorn instead.

#8 YOU ARE GOOD ENOUGH, AFTER ALL

I know that to some people, I seem the tiniest bit arrogant. But like most people, I've always wrestled with some form of the eternal question:

Am I good enough?

When I was twenty-four, I worked at a radio station in Columbus, Ohio. I was doing really well, chipping away at our competitor's ratings, until eventually, we were beating them consistently.

I got a call from a big station in Philadelphia, Pennsylvania. Making the jump from Columbus to Philadelphia would have been huge for anyone, but especially for someone in their early twenties. I flew to meet the manager of the Philadelphia station and spent a weekend touring the station and the city.

Finally, it was just the two of us at lunch. The job was mine if I wanted it. The money was great and the team seemed like they had a good shot at winning in the ratings.

I balked. I was honest. I told him I wasn't sure I was ready to do mornings in Philadelphia. Heck, I was only twenty-four and had been doing morning radio for less than three years! "I'm not up for this!" I proclaimed.

"Dave," he said in a mentoring tone. "I've wondered if I'm good enough to be here. Everyone wonders if they're good enough. We all think someone's going to notice we're incompetent and unfit to be in a great job and we get nervous about it. I'm here to tell you, you are ready for this job."

I listened carefully and soaked in his wise words.

And then I totally ignored them. I was still convinced I wasn't ready for Philadelphia. I went back to Columbus where I was comfortable and didn't have anything to prove. I spent three more years in Columbus, having a great time absolutely murdering our competition. It was easy and it was fun to win the ratings battle month after month.

I don't think I necessarily made a mistake by turning down the Philly job, but I DO know that I turned it down for the wrong reason. Usually people turn down jobs because they don't want to leave their family, the money isn't right, or they don't want to live somewhere else. Me, I was not living near family in Ohio, the money in Philly was double what I was making, and depending on who you ask, the city of Philadelphia is considerably more awesome than the city of Columbus. I turned the job down solely because of what I thought of myself. Looking back, I realize if that station wanted me, if I had a good track record, and if I had believed in myself, then I WAS good enough.

YOU are good enough. How do I know? Well, I don't. But if you're wondering if you are, then chances are good

YOU are good enough.

that yep, you really are. So take that new job. Apply for that new position. Enter that contest. Ask that person out. So what if you fail? Would you have succeeded if you *didn't* try?

#9 YOUR SMILE IS PRETTY IMPORTANT

I know a wonderful woman with crooked teeth. In every photo, instead of a happy, toothy smile, she gives that tight-lipped, fake-looking smile. I feel badly for her because she knows her teeth look just awful, so she doesn't like to smile.

I could tell you that it's what's on the inside that matters, but I'm going to shoot straight instead. Get your teeth fixed. No matter how much it costs, it's worth it, at any age. The orthodontist will even set up a payment plan for you. If you don't smile because your teeth are crooked, then you'll look cranky all the time. I know it's not cheap, but if we can afford tattoos, booze, and cigarettes, we can definitely put some money toward our smiles.

#10 DON'T WORRY ABOUT IT

Scott Dunkin was the best friend any kid could ever ask for.

In the winter of my third-grade year, I got kicked out of the school Christmas pageant on the first day of practice. The music teacher clearly stated that anyone who screwed around would be removed from the show. Immediately after, she busted me dancing while trying to make my buddies laugh. When the other kids rehearsed, I sat on a bench outside the principal's office doing nothing. I was *so* bored.

That same week, my best friend, Scott, made the ultimate sacrifice. He purposely acted up in rehearsal and got kicked out of the pageant too. Every day for a couple of weeks, we'd sit there on the bench, hearing "Deck the Halls" echo down the hallway. If I wasn't allowed in this epic, magical Christmas production, at least I didn't have to sit on the bench alone. The day of the pageant, Scott and I watched all the moms and dads file into the gym to watch the show.

Worrying does about as much good as *not* worrying, so why bother wasting the time?

Scott was a great friend. I remember one thing he taught me, which still serves me to this day. Whenever I'd get stressed about something, Scott would say in a laid-back, drawn-out way, "Don't *w o r r y* about it." No matter how bad I made any problem out to be, he'd pause for a thoughtful second and then repeat, "Don't *w o r r y* about it."

At sixteen, Scott was wise beyond his years. Worrying does about as much good as *not* worrying, so why bother wasting the time?

I haven't seen Scott Dunkin since we were both about twenty years old, but whenever I start to worry about something, I can hear him saying, "Don't *w o r r y* about it!"

#11 YOU PROBABLY *CAN'T* SING

Most of us think we're pretty good singers. Most of us are wrong.

Why is this even important to know? If you've watched *American Idol*, you know how many people want to be the next big singing sensation. People are absolutely shocked when the judges don't see their talent. Some feel dejected and say, "But everyone tells me that I am a great singer." Others say in anger, "No one can tell me I can't do something! I'm going to keep chasing my dream no matter what you say!"

The best thing that could happen to these future car-wash employees is to realize that they can't sing well enough to make a living doing it. That way, they could focus on, oh, I don't know, maybe taking online classes to learn an actual skill that could land them an actual job.

But of course, there are people who *can* sing. I think the way you can tell if you are a good singer is if people tell you unsolicited, "Wow! You really have a great talent!" And when I say "people," I mean someone other than your parents or your best friend.

Instead of wasting years chasing the dream of becoming a singer with no evidence that you can sing, find out what you do well and gravitate toward that. At the same time, learn what you suck at and stay *far* away. Me? I can't dance. I never could. And you'll never see me trying.

#12 COACH YOUR KID'S SOCCER TEAM

I've never played soccer outside of gym class in junior high. So when my six-year-old daughter's soccer team needed a coach, I was the worst possible choice. I did it anyway. Do you want to know why? Because no other parent volunteered! As you probably guessed, our team sucked. I think we scored one goal all season. One. Goal. All. Season. The other parents knew they couldn't complain about my coaching. They didn't offer to coach, after all. I noticed a similar problem when my son was in Cub Scouts. Like in most organizations, the same three people did 99 percent of the work.

It amazes me there are parents who never even *consider* helping out. Hey, she's your kid. You probably should help out with some of her activities. You don't have to be an expert camper or a former pro baseball player to lead a bunch of kids. Just being a good, reliable, and helpful person is enough. Besides, your kids are growing up fast. You might as well help out with their activities so you can spend a little more time with them.

#13 IT'S BETTER TO HAVE IT AND NOT NEED IT THAN TO NEED IT AND NOT HAVE IT

I don't know where my dad got this expression but he used to regularly piss me off by saying it.

Going camping? "Dave, it might rain. You should take your poncho." I'd mumble some reason not to, usually because it was too much effort to find it and put it in my backpack. Then here it came, "Better to have it and not *blah*, *blah*, *blah*."

Of course, he was right. Two days later I'd be shivering in some remote wilderness, looking like I had just gotten out of a washing machine, wishing I'd brought the stupid poncho. If it hadn't rained, it wouldn't have been a big deal. I would have just left my poncho in my backpack.

Like most parents, I use my dad's annoying lines on my kids now. My son will head out the door with no jacket to a Friday-night high-school football game. "You better take a hoodie, Carson," I'll remind him.

"I don't need one, Dad. It's warm out," he protests.

This is where I feel it is my time to shine. "Well, it might get cold later and it's better to have it and not need it than to need it and not have it!" I say it as if it is the most profound nugget of wisdom ever spoken.

I know it pisses my son off, but he'll be saying it to his kids one day, I'm sure of that.

#14 IF YOU PLAY WITH FIRE, YOU'RE GOING TO GET BURNED

I'm a bad listener because of my mom.

Mom talked *constantly* when I was a kid, even if no one was listening. I had to learn to shut her out just to do my homework. Today, you have to tell me something about seven times before I finally hear you. Thanks, Mom!

Mom did say one thing that sank in. For years I had no idea what it meant. She'd say, "If you play with fire, you're going to get burned." I thought it was nonsense she'd utter whenever my brother or sisters and I got into trouble.

Later, I learned interpretations to that saying, such as, "If you have sex with a girl, you're going to get her pregnant." I discovered soon enough that was an accurate interpretation.

Mom's advice might have been hard for a ten-year-old kid to understand, but we adults know exactly what she

If you screw around with something you shouldn't, it's probably going to bite you in the ass.

meant. If you screw around with something you shouldn't, it's probably going to bite you in the ass. Trying to break open an ATM with a sledgehammer might sound like a good idea, but chances are pretty good it will be regrettable. Taunting your neighbor's Rottweiler sounds like harmless fun, but it can lead to some major discomfort down the road. And yes, having meaningless sex actually can make a baby and all the permanent fun that comes with it.

#15 GET RID OF BULLSHIT THOUGHTS THAT HOLD YOU BACK

I was in eighth-grade art class when I overheard two girls talking about me.

"He's so ugly, he looks like a monkey!"

I knew I wasn't like Jeff Helweg, the cutest boy in school, but I never thought I looked like a monkey. Right there in art class, on that very day, I learned the truth. Ouch.

For the rest of my school years, I didn't talk to girls because I figured they wouldn't want to talk to some

kid who looked like a monkey. I never went to prom or homecoming or even school dances. I never had a date until halfway through my senior year because I was too afraid of getting rejected on account of my ugliness.

Sometime after high school, when girls started actually voluntarily talking to me, flirting with me, and even wanting to make out with me, I realized that maybe I wasn't as ugly as I'd imagined all those years. Maybe I wasn't anywhere near Jeff Helweg's league, but did I actually look like a monkey? Probably not, I decided. The possibility occurred to me later that those girls in art class might not have even been talking about me! Sadly, the belief that I was ugly made me miss a lot of fun in high school.

When my grandma was about five, her mom had a friend over to visit. Grandma, being a typical little girl, tried her best to show off for her mom's visitor, speaking five-year-old nonsense just to get attention.

"Be quiet! No one wants to hear what you have to say!" her mom snapped.

Those words stuck with my grandma for the rest of her life. She became very shy. She always questioned whether her words had any value to anyone and most of the time she decided it was better if she just kept quiet.

Poor Grandma. She took her mother's impatient words as truth and that single belief limited so much potential joy and confidence in her life. If her mom hadn't said those damn words, who knows how many more friends and conversations Grandma would have had throughout the years. How many times was her opinion not heard because she believed no one wanted to hear what she had to say?

What do you know to be true about yourself? Do you know that you have an annoying laugh? A dull personality? Nothing to offer a potential partner? Wait a second. Do you know this for *certain,* or are you like my grandma and me?

Get rid of whatever bullshit idea holds you back in life. Think about how much better your life would be if you found out that you'd been wrong the whole time!

#16 NEVER GIVE UP—UNLESS IT'S TIME

Winston Churchill was once asked to speak to a group of students. It seemed as though he didn't have anything prepared. Churchill stood up, walked to the podium, paused for effect, and said, "Never, ever, ever give up." Then he sat down.

Churchill was famous for not giving up. During the darkest days of World War II, Germany was pretty much annihilating Great Britain from the sky. Planes dropped bombs while primitive, poorly aimed rockets fell on both military and civilian targets. The entire population lived in fear. In fact, the whole "Keep Calm and Carry On" campaign was a creation of the British government at the time in hopes of somehow calming the nerves of the people.

Prime Minister Churchill eventually was able to turn the tide in World War II, and with the help of the United States, beat the snot out of Germany. Churchill knew a thing or two about never giving up.

Fast-forward twenty-five years. As told in the book and movie *The Wrecking Crew*, a young guitar player in Los Angeles begged to take lessons from one of the best guitarists in the city. The guitarist insisted he didn't give lessons, but he finally gave in. After months of lessons and tireless practice, the student asked, "Do I have what it takes to be a great guitarist?"

The answer was both honest and simple. "No. No, you'll never be a great guitarist."

With that, the student gave up guitar. But instead of a life of obscurity, he took a new direction. He went on to become one of the greatest music producers of the 1960s, influencing music in a way that still resonates in much of the music we hear today. His name was Phil Spector.

One more story about never giving up. Years ago, a radio friend of mine was diagnosed with cancer. His doctors didn't see much hope and gave him the "Get your affairs in order" talk. "Screw that!" said my friend. He got other doctors to examine him and sure enough, not only was there hope, but fifteen years later, he's still alive and as big a pain in the ass as ever. He could have given up, but he didn't.

"Never give up" sounds all noble and everything, but sometimes it's best to cut your losses and start over fresh. If you hire someone who's not working out, it would be stupid to say, "I'll never give up on him!" Nope, cut your losses, turn the page, and show him the door. After all, it's in his best interest to go somewhere he can flourish.

Maybe you know someone with a dream of being a great stand-up comic. And ten years later, he's still looking for his first paying gig. If it's just for fun, great! But if he's still living in mom's basement while waiting for a call from the Laff Hut in Missoula, then it might be time to help him refocus his energy.

Churchill didn't have the luxury of giving up. For him it was a matter of life and death. My friend with cancer *could* have given up, but he didn't. Phil Spector chose to

---

Sometimes it's best to cut your losses and start over fresh.

---

give up his dream because he could see it was time to find another passion. These are all great examples.

Never give up. Unless it's time.

#17 YOUR PET IS NOT AS AWESOME AS YOU THINK

I love pets. I've been the proud and somewhat conscientious owner of everything from a dog that holds records for shedding to a tortoise that (no one warned me!) would grow to the size of a basketball.

There isn't much for me to complain about with pets because I'm pretty tolerant of them. They're nicer than most people and rarely ask to borrow money. I've never had a beagle call me from jail at two in the morning!

I don't mind when someone's dog jumps up at me when I visit. I don't mind when their cat climbs onto my lap. I've even been known to encourage dogs to hump my leg by giving them suggestive looks and putting gravy in my cuffs.

But not everyone is like me when it comes to pets. Lots of pet owners let their cute little "Rottie" (short for "Don't Piss Them Off Because They Can Surgically Remove Your Face") jump all over you when you walk in

the door. They'll say, "Oh, he likes you! I hope you don't mind!" Of course you lie and say something about how awesome it is that he's clawing you up with scars that might never fade.

I'm guilty of being "that guy" myself. Years ago, I lived in a condo and shared a yard with a few neighbors. Since I figured no one would mind (dumb mistake), I let my dog use our yard as a giant, grassy toilet. One day I came home to a grocery bag full of dog poop on my front porch. MY dog's poop. I wasn't even mad. I felt more embarrassed than anything else.

But that's just the start of what some people's pets do to annoy us. We have Owner Who Does Not Pick Up Poop While On a Walk, Dog Who Barks Constantly, and Dog Who Harasses My Cat/Wife/Son/Mailman.

People sometimes forget that they're among the few who really appreciate their pet. It's kind of like how people are convinced that their rotten kids are gifted, special, and misunderstood. I know Buddy the drooling bulldog's owners love him, but the rest of us might opt out of getting covered in hair and dog snot if we had a choice.

#18 DON'T TALK LIKE YOU'RE HALF-ASLEEP

People judge us on our appearance. But when they can't see us, they look for another way to judge us. How? Our voice. So when you leave a voicemail for someone, don't sound like you're calling from your deathbed. Put a little energy into your voice, so the person you're calling or leaving a voicemail for will picture an actual living person on the phone. I don't care who you are calling, you don't want to sound like someone who hasn't slept in three days.

#19 CRITICS ARE JUST TRYING TO IMPRESS OTHER CRITICS

Chances are good that the guy who writes movie reviews for your local paper was recently promoted from writing obituaries. No, I'm serious. I know a guy who got his big career bump when he was promoted from writing about dead people to telling the readership what movies to see.

His qualifications were pretty much limited to the fact that he could see, hear, catch a bus to the theater, and write coherent sentences. In exchange, he got to rip musicians, TV stars, stand-up comics, and live theater productions.

Case in point: back in 1972, The Rolling Stones released their album *Exile on Main Street*. All the critics hated it. Today, it makes nearly every single top-album-of-all-time list.

Whoops.

You're better off asking your friends for movie recommendations.

To be fair, there are critics, some in my own city, who do know what they're talking about. I don't know what originally qualified Roger Ebert as a critic, but he seemed to get it right more often than not. The guy from your local television station on the other hand? He's just happy he's no longer doing the traffic reports at 6:00 a.m.

It's cool to show other people how smart we are. Just remember, critics are mostly trying to prove how smart they are to other critics. Let them do that. Just don't waste much of *your* time with them. You're better off asking your friends for movie recommendations.

#20 DON'T SIT ON YOUR GREAT IDEA

I remember exactly where I was when I had the most amazing idea. I was driving out of downtown Minneapolis on the freeway when it hit me. I would write a best-selling book.

I got started on my book idea right away and worked hard on it for about a year. I interviewed more than one hundred people and got some phenomenal stories. I even worked to pitch the concept to some publishers to see if they were interested. The downside to talking to so many people about my book is that it was impossible to keep what I was doing a secret.

Here's where I screwed up. I got a little bored and a little frustrated with the grueling task of making the book fresh and interesting. Yes, the stories themselves were fascinating, but I had trouble with how to present them in the best way possible. I stopped working on it for a while. I thought a month or two off would give me a renewed passion for finishing the manuscript. When a few months turned into a year, and then a few years turned into a long time, that's when things went south for me.

One weekend morning, long after "taking a short break" from my book, I was watching television. An author was being interviewed about his new book. All I could do was drop my jaw and stare at the screen in front of me. The book was so similar to my book that it simply could not be a coincidence. Somehow, he'd heard from someone I'd talked to about my idea and beat me to it.

I don't blame him; I blame me. After all, *I* was the one who blew it. I had a huge head start. It was my book to finish. I knew I couldn't just blow it off indefinitely. But that's pretty much what I did. I'd blown it and had no one to blame but myself.

They say that everyone who has ever taken a shower has gotten a great idea in there, but it's the person who gets out of the shower and *acts* on their idea who has success.

Don't sit on your great idea. Think about how awesome you'll feel when you see it become reality. Work on it every single day until you make it happen. Remember, if you don't, someone else will.

#21 SHOVEL AN OLD PERSON'S DRIVEWAY

Minnesota is known to get about fifty inches of snow every winter. Even if you're lucky enough to have a snow blower, clearing your driveway and sidewalk is a lot of work. As hard as it is for you, it's even harder on old people. Instead of watching out your window as your eighty-seven-year-old neighbor, Elmer, tries to get his walk shoveled before cardiac arrest does him in, put down your Leinenkugel and help him out. Even better, beat Elmer to it and use your fancy new Toro on his walk so he can stare out his window at *you* for a change.

Don't expect anything in return. When you're old, hopefully someone will do the same for you.

#22 SPELL CHECK AND AUTOCORRECT ARE GREAT FEATURES, BUT . . .

It's not a big deal when you're texting your good friend, "Meat me at the library. Ill sea you their."

The problem with spelling like a slow third grader is that it becomes a familiar way of life until one day, you'll need to make a good impression with a prospective employer. If your cover letter says, "I'll be looking forward too meating you," you will never hear from them.

If you're writing an impassioned letter to a small business owner, you'll look like a blathering idiot when you say, "Your gonna make alot of peeple angrey if you closed down that porn shop!"

Anything written with bad spelling is about as persuasive as listening to someone speak with a hunk of spinach in their front teeth. They just can't be taken seriously because all you see is that spinach.

#23 THE MAN WHO DOESN'T READ GOOD BOOKS IS NO BETTER OFF THAN THE MAN WHO CANNOT

Mark Twain said that. It goes for women too.

#24 ELIMINATE EVERY OTHER POSSIBILITY

Growing up, I never showed any signs of ever amounting to much. I was an average student, did my fair share of partying, and took every sloppy shortcut that I could, no matter what the task.

Sometimes I reflect on my career in radio and feel

pretty amazed that it worked out for me. For someone who was a slacker as a kid, I'm so happy I found a career that interested me. And I think part of the reason for my success in radio is that I purposely eliminated every other possible career choice at an early age.

When I was about sixteen, we took a career aptitude test at school. We've all taken these career placement surveys. Answer a few dozen questions and the computer would spit out whether you'd be suited for a career as a doctor or a doorman, an engineer or a hair stylist.

Since I pretty much rocked at cheating on tests, I decided to cheat on this one too. For every question, I'd think about how I'd answer if I already worked at a radio station, the one and only career dream I'd ever had.

"Do you like working outdoors?" No. (Even though I do.)

"Do you like working with tools and equipment?" Yes. (As long as it was radio equipment.)

"Do you enjoy doing physical labor?" (Hell no.)

Sure enough, my scheme worked. At the very top of the list of career recommendations: Radio Announcer. Perfect.

A few months later, I was enrolled in Radio and TV Broadcasting at Pikes Peak Community College in Colorado Springs. To my mom and dad's utter astonishment, I got nothing but straight A's!

I had no idea what a favor I was doing for myself by cheating on that career placement test. But, if you get rid of all the other distracting possibilities in front of you, it's almost unavoidable to be *really good* at that one thing. It could be radio, tennis, calculus, painting, or cooking. Sure, it helps to have some natural ability in the first place, but if you do? Wow! You'll be amazed at what you can do once you get all that other crap out of your mind!

#25 ONLY A SIXTEEN-YEAR-OLD COULD WRITE A SONG LIKE THAT

In 2013, the songs "Royals" and "Team" by New Zealand singer and songwriter Lorde were huge pop hits. Let's face it: they were both strange as hell. The weird harmonies, vocals, and lyrics were like nothing I'd ever heard before in my life. And as a radio deejay, I've heard *a lot* of music.

Sure, there's a bunch of great new music out there, so what's so special about these songs? They're in a class of their own because no thirty-five-year-old could have written them. How do I know? Because once we get to a certain age, we put rules on ourselves. We are careful not to step out of bounds and risk offending others or open ourselves up to ridicule. From Coldplay to Luke Bryan, it's pretty safe. Their music is great, but their songs are not drastically different from a thousand other artists' songs out there.

But Lorde, who was fifteen and sixteen when she wrote these songs, wasn't restricted by any of these rules. She got away with unconventional harmonies and risky melodies and wrote lyrics about how they grew up poor, but tried to be rich. Lorde was like you and me when we were sixteen. We didn't know any better either. Then we grew up and learned what was expected of us and how and when to fall in line with expectations. We stopped taking those chances that could get us in trouble or make us stand out. Sure enough, we learned to be about as predictable as a Hollywood divorce. There's something refreshing about the way a sixteen-year-old thinks.

When I was about fourteen, my brother-in-law, who was in the Air Force, gave me an old parachute. "They were throwing these away down at the base, and I figured you'd find some use for it," he said, with a look that told me he knew I'd probably kill myself, but to have fun in the process.

A parachute in the hands of a fourteen-year-old boy is a magical thing. It was only about the size of a bed sheet, not big enough to jump off the roof with, but I came up with something almost as thrilling. I bundled this parachute up into the seat of my bike and rigged a ripcord on my handlebar. I rode to the top of a big hill on the gravel road and took off. I pedaled as hard as I could until I was at maximum velocity. At that exact moment, I reached for the ripcord.

What exactly went wrong is still a mystery.

The next thing I knew, I was tangled in a mass of nylon, metal, and flesh, skidding over the rough gravel surface, leaving tiny bits of myself sticking to the road. I still have scars from that adventure.

The funny thing is I had never stopped to think, "Is this a good idea?" or "What would Mom say?" Much like Lorde, I was too young to consider the idea that this kind of thing *just isn't done.*

We all know what happens when we get older. We see an opportunity that seems exciting. We're about ready to take the plunge when it hits us. *Wait*, we think. *What if this goes really, really wrong?*

Caution is a good thing, but not if it shuts down every opportunity for adventure.

Caution is a good thing, but not if it shuts down every opportunity for adventure. Sure, something *can* go wrong in almost anything we do, but that's not a good excuse to put on a helmet and stay in bed all day. It's safe, but there's no chance of success, fun, thrills, romance, or any of those other wonderful things we crave.

What if we forgot the rules once in a while? Find that sixteen-year-old that still lives inside you somewhere and let him or her make the decisions for a day. If you don't get arrested or catch chlamydia, you might be amazed at what happens. And if you're a sixteen-year-old reading this book, don't be in such a rush to grow up. Enjoy being sixteen and all the inexperience that goes with it. You'll miss that inexperience when it's gone.

#26 HIGH SCHOOL IS OVER, PEOPLE

Why is high school such a big deal? Even years after we get our diploma, we still think about high school. If we were either popular or great athletes in high school, we love to relive that. If we wandered the hallways unnoticed or got picked last for dodgeball, we dream of going back and showing everyone how awesome we are now.

I was the latter. I didn't hate high school; I just didn't love it. I was too shy to talk to girls. I hung out with my dopey buddies in the library, got average grades, and had bad skin.

After I got out of high school, I started to make a bit of a transformation. Over the course of a few years, I grew in confidence. I was proud to say I could actually hold a conversation with a woman. My skin even cleared up. I have no idea why, but I found myself wishing I could go back to high school to show everyone there was more to me than the library nerd who dressed funny and broke out in a sweat when a girl talked to him.

So when my high school reunion rolled around, I jumped at the chance to volunteer to emcee the whole thing. I would show everyone who didn't notice me in school that yeah, I was now a badass radio deejay who wore expensive shoes and had a hot wife.

People don't come to their high school reunion to check up on people they didn't originally care about.

I emceed the shit out of that reunion. I was funny, charming, and professional, not to mention my teeth had never looked so white! My wife looked hot and I wasn't intimidated by anyone.

You know what? Nobody even cared. People don't come to their high school reunion to check up on people they didn't originally care about. They come to see what happened to the ones they *did* care about. And everyone is simultaneously trying to show off. I might have proved to everyone that I am not a geek anymore, but it didn't matter. After that weekend, I left high school where it belongs: in the past.

#27 WE'RE ABOUT AS HAPPY AS WE DECIDE TO BE

I know a guy who is dying of multiple sclerosis (MS). He's barely able to get around and uses a scooter because it's just too hard for him to walk. But when I talk to him, he *never* mentions his physical pain. He's just too damn *happy* to bitch and moan about his circumstances.

By contrast, I know plenty of people who are always *unhappy*. I don't dare ask how they're doing because I'll get a laundry list of all the ways the world has screwed them over, how they have rotten friends, and how much they hate their jobs.

Hands down, my friend with MS has it much worse. The difference is that he's decided to be happy. No matter what good things happen to unhappy people, they'll find the crappy side of it. They get a new job, but it's *too* far from home and the traffic is always bad. They have a healthy new baby, but he's *so* much work. They lost forty pounds, but now they *have* to spend extra money on new clothes. Something is always wrong for these people.

We're all guilty. We wait for something to happen to make us happy. We wait for the perfect partner. We wait for that promotion. We wait for the kids to grow up and move out. We wait for the day we can afford that perfect vacation. We think, *Then, I'll be happy*. The problem is there's always something else that would make us happier. I don't claim to have all the answers, but it seems that happy people have just *decided* that's how they want to be.

Some guy named Abe Lincoln once said, *"Most folks are about as happy as they make up their minds to be."* I think he was right.

#28 HAVE SOMETHING TO LOOK FORWARD TO

There are plenty of things in life to dread: work, going to the dentist, Thanksgiving with the in-laws, dying in a fiery Laundromat accident.

To counteract the dreaded things in life, it's nice to have something to look forward to—something that gets you out of bed in the morning.

I try to sprinkle things into my daily life that I can look forward to. It doesn't have to be something big like a trip or buying a new car. It can be as simple as picking up an over-priced cup of coffee at Starbucks on the way to work, watching my favorite fake reality show before falling asleep, or getting a "massage" at that shady place near the bus station.

#29 FOR GUYS ONLY: LIFT THE SEAT BEFORE YOU PEE

Many years ago, I went to an ex-girlfriend's house. I don't remember why, but probably to try to get her back in the sack. While I was there, I went to use the bathroom and there was pee all over the toilet seat. Since she lived there alone, and girls don't usually get pee on the toilet seat, I knew it was from some idiot guy she was seeing.

"You're dating a guy who's so lame that he pees on the toilet seat and doesn't even wipe it off?" I yelled from the bathroom with a hint of ridicule and disgust in my voice. "You can do better than that!"

Not long after that, she dumped him. I think she realized that an adult male who pees on the toilet seat is probably a dumbass in other areas of his life, too.

We're not six anymore, guys. Put that seat up and wipe off anything that misses.

#30 FOR GUYS ONLY: ONE SKILL YOU SHOULD HAVE

I've always admired the guy who can sit down and entertain everyone by playing the nearby piano. Wow, is that ever a cool skill! Find an old upright at a school or a hotel lobby and he can sit down and bang out "The Entertainer" by Scott Joplin, "Music Box Dancer" by Frank Mills, or "Don't Stop Believin'" by Journey.

If you're not already an amazing piano player, you never will be. You're much too busy. If you had great musical ability sitting dormant inside you, it would have shown itself by now. Settle for being able to find a good radio station on your car radio.

The good news is that the one skill every guy should have is one skill every guy can learn. Not only will it impress, but it will also come in handy. Learn to build a fire.

Accidental fires start all the time, but just try starting a fire on purpose. Maybe it sounds easy, but unless you've tried to do it lately, you probably don't realize it's kind of tricky. You might get some bundle of paper started with no problem, but getting those bigger pieces to catch isn't as simple as it sounds. You can have an entire Sunday

New York Times and a pile of dry leaves and *still* be unsuccessful.

I'm not going to tell you how to build a fire here. You can go on YouTube and find all kinds of helpful tutorials. What I will say is that the next time you're at a cabin during a snowstorm, you will be the big hero when you build a blazing fire for your friends.

And that's almost as impressive as playing the piano.

#31 FOR GUYS ONLY: YOU'RE PROBABLY ABOUT AVERAGE IN BED

Most guys are not great in bed. But every man *thinks* he's an amazing lover. Why?

I think I know the answer: women are not honest about their experience. They will even fake an orgasm just to get their partner to stop.

I'm not here to attempt to give you any advice on how to improve your sex life. That's what online porn is for. I'm only doing my best to bring you back down to earth when it comes to your sexual prowess.

Guys, she's had better, but don't worry about it. She's also had worse.

#32 FOR WOMEN ONLY: NEVER DYE YOUR HAIR RED

It never looks natural. Even women who swear their new red hair looks natural, it doesn't. Red hair is impossible to recreate artificially. Plus, real redheads have the skin, eyes, and facial structure to go along with their hair. Go blond, but never go red, unless that *unnatural* look is what you're going for.

#33 FOR WOMEN ONLY: THERE'S A REASON YOUR FRIENDS DON'T LIKE THAT GUY

Our friends put up with a lot from us to keep us happy, whether it be going to restaurants just because *we* want to go there, sitting through *Love Actually* with us for the

thirty-seventh time, or pretending to like our boyfriend or girlfriend even if they don't.

But once in a while, your friends won't like your boyfriend. They'll even tell you, "This guy is an idiot! He makes you pay for everything, he hit on me while you were in the bathroom, and he talks with his mouth open!"

"What? We are so in love!" you say. "I just love how his food flies everywhere when he talks! It's so *cute*!"

There's a lot of stuff that's *cute* when we're falling in love. You might think it's adorable that he lives with his mom and has a warrant out for his arrest, but your friends aren't "in love" with him, so they can plainly see that he's an asshole.

Remember when your mom and dad didn't like you hanging out with that one kid when you were little? You know, the one who later went to rehab fourteen times and now works at the gas station? Well, it's kind of like that. Your parents, just like your friends, tend to want you to have a good life, and they think staying away from habitual idiots is a key to your happiness. When your friends or parents tell you that your new flame is a loser, ignore them at your own peril. Either way, you'll find out they were right sooner or later.

#34 FOR WOMEN ONLY: YOUR HAIRSTYLE LOOKED GREAT WHEN YOU WERE IN HIGH SCHOOL

Not so much now.

I'm not sure why so many forty-five-year-old women still wear the exact same style they wore in high school. I mean, this has to be a very deliberate decision, right? They actually get out of the shower and knowingly do their hair the same way they did when New Kids on the Block had a bunch of hits.

I've seen enough makeovers on *The Today Show* to realize that an old hairstyle makes anyone look old. Take the plunge, get a new hairstyle, and don't look back.

Part 2

Show up on TIME

#35 SHOW UP ON TIME

"Eighty percent of success is showing up."

—Well-Known Celebrity Sleazebag

Okay, the guy who said this (and maybe you know who it is) isn't exactly a pillar of society, but he *did* get this right. Forgive me?

It's no mystery. You can't get anything done if you're not there to do it. Besides, showing up late is rude, selfish, and completely pisses off everyone who got there on time.

I know a guy who got fired because he just couldn't show up on time. I mean, he could if there was something in it for him, but he usually just didn't bother.

You can't get anything done if you're not there to do it.

Look, *everyone* is late once in a while. We all get a pass there. But if people have to tell you to be somewhere at six o'clock, hoping you'll show up at least by seven o'clock, that shit ain't cute. If this describes you, it's time to grow up.

#36 FEED THE GOAT

My first radio job wasn't even at a *cool* radio station, but I didn't care. We played religious music and I barely got to talk on the radio, but I was still thrilled!

My new boss, Mr. Boles, was showing me around the radio station. Like most new hires, I was hearing about half of what he was saying while I was thinking about things that were important to ME. I was thinking about how cute the receptionist was, what kind of snacks were in the candy machine, and how far the men's room was from the studio.

Suddenly, Mr. Boles led me outside where we stood at the foot of the radio antenna. As I blinked in the bright sunlight, he explained that one of my duties would be feeding Rita.

It slowly dawned on me that Rita was the goat that was staring back at me. I remember thinking, *There is no way in hell that a big radio star like me is gonna feed a goat. And hey, why is there a goat here anyway?* It turns out the goat's job was to keep the grass trimmed around all the high voltage stuff that sat at the foot of the antenna.

Later that day, I told my dad in disgust about the menial duty of taking care of a barnyard animal as part of my glamorous new radio job. "Well," he said, "if you don't do it, they'll find someone who will. And since you have to do it anyway, you might as well learn to like it."

When I thought about it, feeding the goat was a small price to pay for getting my first real break in radio. So I fed the goat. I watered the damn thing too. And during super-long pipe-organ mega-mixes on the radio, I'd even come outside and give Rita a scratch or two. It turned out that feeding the goat wasn't so bad after all.

Six months later, when a better radio job opened up, Mr. Boles recommended me for it and I got the job! Doing what I was expected to do at my job without complaining paid off!

You might not ever be asked to feed a goat in your career, but that goat will appear in some form or another. You'll get asked to work on a holiday or you'll be asked to keep the company van washed. When that happens, you can bitch and moan about how "they don't pay me enough to do that!" Most people do. Or you can just do it, knowing that it's got to be done, and maybe, just maybe, someone is going to notice. Just feed the goat.

#37 LEARN TO TYPE

As far as practical skills go, typing is right up there with bathing, lying, and talking your way out of a speeding ticket.

Typing, or "keyboarding," as they call it in schools now, will serve you well. If you don't know how, don't avoid it. Just learn. There are some great free websites that offer games for practicing your typing skills. And if you don't have a computer with a real keyboard attached, visit your local library and use a computer there.

#38 YOU CAN LEARN SOMETHING FROM EVERY BOSS

One of the best bosses I ever had was only twenty-four years old. He was only four years older than me at the time, so what could I possibly learn from him? Turned out he was friendly and fun, and at the same time, he was professional. I remember one time when several of us deejays were sitting around talking about how to land wedding deejay gigs to make extra income. Without being totally rude, he said, "I think it's better if you discuss this outside of work because you all have plenty to do here."

Wow, great point! Here we were on the clock, scheming on how to make money with a second job. Was it a horrible sin? Not really, but he reminded us that maybe we'd be better off if we got back to work on our primary job.

You won't always learn great behaviors from your boss. I had another boss, also twenty-four years old, who used to let underage girls sit on his lap and run the control board during his radio show. I am not making this up. And if it weren't bad enough already, he was married. He was later fired. I'm pretty sure I would have figured out not to do this on my own, but he definitely sped up the learning process for me.

BEST BOSS

Another boss loved doing cocaine with his buddies at work and hiring hot young women so he could have sex with them. He was married too. Unbelievably, he was promoted, and the entire staff resented him for it.

You'll have several bosses during your career. Some will be amazing and some will have you wondering why no one else sees their stupidity. And you know what? You can learn something from each one of them.

#39 SOMETIMES YOU HAVE TO MOVE OUT TO MOVE UP

If you've listened to my radio show, *The Dave Ryan Show*, on KDWB 101.3, you probably remember a guy named Crisco. That wasn't his real name, of course. His name was Adam. He earned the name Crisco when he worked at a sandwich shop and got fired when he was caught on a security camera throwing knives at cans of cooking oil.

Crisco worked at KDWB for ten years but never got offered a full-time job. Why? It's because we always looked at him as that lovable screw-up who created a sea of cooking oil at his old job. To me, he was a great guy and a good friend (he still is), but not the type that should be promoted.

First impressions are hard to overcome.

So Crisco left.

And good for him for doing that. He got a fresh start with a group of people who saw him differently. That's all he needed. They didn't see him for what he had been, but for what he could become.

First impressions are hard to overcome. And you don't have to throw knives at cans of cooking oil to make a bad first impression. You'll make your first impression within the first couple of days and weeks on a new job. Chances are, three years later, you'll still be thought of exactly the same way.

So follow Crisco's lead and leave. There's another company out there that'll see you as you are now, not as you were back when you started. Just don't mess up this time!

#40 THAT'S NOT MY JOB

And its evil twin: "They don't pay me enough to do that."

Of course they don't. They never will until you show that you don't mind doing it.

Pretty much every person I've worked with who uttered one of these two phrases got let go in the next round of layoffs. They're now happily lounging around

About 90 percent of the people at any workplace do just enough to keep their job.

at the car wash, playing on their phone, and muttering, "That's not my job," while someone else is doing all the work. Don't let these phrases leave your tongue.

We had a new intern at our radio station and her first assignment was to go to a big concert, hand out T-shirts, blow up balloons, and hang up KDWB banners. When told of this assignment, she said, "I'm not doing any *bitch* work."

Wait … *WHAT?*

She shouldn't have looked at it as anything other than an opportunity to put her ambition on display.

The way I figure, about 90 percent of the people at any workplace do just enough to keep their job, and not a bit more.

When high schools and colleges ask me to come speak about careers or success or radio or STDs, I throw this little gem out there: all you have to do is work a little harder than you are expected to and you'll be a standout. Work a LOT harder than you are expected to and you will be a total rock star. You might think I'm not serious, but give it a try.

#41 PRAISE YOUR EMPLOYEES

Your employees love their paycheck. It helps them buy food, scratch lottery tickets, and buy a nice suit to wear to interview for a better job.

You know what they love even more than their paychecks? They love being told they're doing a good job. So if they are, for the love of God, praise them for their good work!

I've worked for bosses who must have thought if they said anything nice to an employee, it would go straight to her head and make her unmanageable.

Boss: "Great job on getting more of our chemicals into juice boxes, Pete! This is really going to help our bottom line!"

Pete: "Why thank you! Since I'm so wonderful and valuable now, I'm going to start coming in late and sleeping with your daughter!"

Boss: (to himself) "Wow, I should have never told Pete he was doing a good job. I'll certainly never do *that* again!"

I know this conversation seems ludicrous, but I swear some bosses must think this is what would happen if they praised their employees!

We all love to feel like we are making a difference. I even read an article that said employees rate "feeling valued" higher in importance than the dollar amount of their paycheck. Of course, that sounds like complete bullshit to some of us, but a little pat on the back once in a while sure feels nice. If you are a boss, don't be afraid to praise your employees. Watch for results. You'll be amazed.

#42 NEVER FIND OUT WHAT YOUR CO-WORKERS GET PAID

Everybody thinks they want to know what their co-workers get paid.

But you really don't want to know. It's kind of like hearing how a magician makes a girl disappear. I mean, wow! It's so cool! One minute she was there in the box, and I swear, the next second she was gone!

But when you find out she clumsily slips out of the box and squats behind it, you find yourself thinking, *I wish I had never asked*.

When you find out how much your co-worker makes, chances are good that you'll be pissed. Even if they make *less* than you, you'll wonder how such an unqualified lazy ass could be making that much. And if they make that

Everybody thinks they want to know
what their co-workers get paid.
But you really don't want to know.

much, certainly *you* should make a whole lot more than you do!

Don't get tempted. Maybe you should talk about which co-workers are sleeping together instead.

#43 AIRPLANE TRAVEL

About carry-on luggage: how come I can get my bag in the overhead compartment and my butt into the seat in six-and-a-half seconds flat while other people take *forever*? It seems like I always get someone in my row who has never been on an airplane before. Please, take the flight attendant's advice and "kindly step out of the aisle."

If I sit next to you, a nice "Hello" is fine, but I'm sorry, I don't really want to talk to you. No offense, but I'd probably rather take a nap than respond to, "So where are you flying to today?" I'm thinking, *Oh, I don't know, maybe the same place you're flying to?* And if I respond with one-word answers, please take the social cue that I'd rather take a nap, watch my movie, or read my copy of *Miniature Donkey Talk* magazine.

About reclining airline seats: For many years, airline passengers have reclined their seats during flight. While it was always a pain for the person behind them, no one complained because they had every right to do it. That's why there's a button on their seat, so they can lean back and enjoy the extra space, even if it's only three-quarters of an inch more.

A few years ago, our self-centered and entitled society started to collectively decide that if the seat in front of them is reclined, it's offensive! Oh, and we LOVE being offended! How dare you touch a button on a seat that *you* paid for and recline into *my* space?

I'm sorry, but if it's my button, then it's actually my space. Your space is behind you, so hit that button, lean back, relax, and shut up.

#44 CELL PHONES

PEOPLE NEED TO STOP TALKING SO %&#@ING LOUD! I know it's hard to believe, but the engineers who made phones actually designed them to be sensitive enough to hear a whisper. Don't believe me? Try it sometime.

There are usually two kinds of people who talk loudly on their cell phones. One is the business guy who is sitting across from you at the airport, loudly informing some poor bastard, "YES! I BOUGHT THEIR ENTIRE INVENTORY OF VIBRATORS! YES! CORRECT, THE ENTIRE INVENTORY. WE'LL MAKE A KILLING ON THOSE IN BIRMINGHAM!"

The other offender is the old person. They were born back when you had to climb a phone pole and dial the operator in order to call the feed store. The idea that this cell phone is capable of transmitting anything but a shout totally escapes them. "Old Country Buffet? YES! I'll meet you there at five o'clock! And how *was* George's GALL BLADDER SURGERY? Uh-oh, you don't say!"

We're not going to change these people. We can only try to avoid becoming like them. So when you get old, or when you run a successful sex toy import-export business, please remember what you learned in this book.

#45 WHY CASINOS HAVE THICK, LUXURIOUS CARPET

I moved to Las Vegas when I was twenty-one. I didn't have an apartment yet, so I stayed for three weeks at the fabulous El Rancho Hotel and Casino. Because I was new in town and didn't know anyone yet, I played a lot of video poker. I'd win, then I'd lose, then I'd win, then I'd lose again. Overall, I lost. What sucked is that I lost my laundry money. Go without laundry money for a couple weeks and you'll regret it. When you find yourself wearing swim trunks as underwear because you gambled away your laundry money, life sucks.

Most of the money you bring into a casino, you end up *giving* to the casino. Sure, once in a while we win a couple hundred dollars on a slot machine or have a great night at the blackjack table, but most of the time, we lose money. And if you are ahead and you choose to keep playing, give it some time because you're eventually going to give back all your winnings.

Go to Vegas. Gamble. Go to shows. Have fun. And when you win, grab that cash, spend part of it on a good buffet, hit the bar for a few drinks, and then go home! Wait, skip the bar, because you'll probably get drunk and go back and drop all the money you just won. On second thought, get out of that casino *fast*!

#46 DON'T BORROW MONEY

It's tempting to hit up your folks for some cash so you can get a newer car, or ask them to cover some of your expenses because you spent too much on that electronic birdbath you couldn't live without. I literally heard  someone in their twenties tell me it was her parents' responsibility to loan her money whenever she needed it because they're the ones who had her. *Huh?*

Listen, I'm not dead set against borrowing money when you really need it, then making it your first priority to pay it back. But too much of the time, people need to borrow money because of bad planning and dumb decisions. I'll bet you know someone who is always broke, even though they have a job. It's just that they cannot hang on to their money. They just *have* to run to the big box store for that new electronic thing. The bigger problem with borrowing money is that you don't feel the pain of your own dumbass decisions. When your parents or someone else bails you out, do you learn anything? Nope.

#47 DON'T LOAN MONEY

It was the last day of sixth grade. Before the teacher would give us our final report card, we had to repay any library fines we had been hit with during the school year. A kid named Jeff was beside himself because he didn't want to go home without that report card, but he needed $1.50 to pay his fine. "Please!"

he begged, almost tearfully, "I swear I'll pay you back the first day of school next year. Please!"

I gave in. After all, he said he'd pay me back and he seemed like he meant it.

I spotted Jeff in the lunch line on the first day of seventh grade. If there's any place where a kid is going to be holding money, it's in the lunch line. So I walked up and asked for my buck fifty. I can still see the smarmy look on his face when he flat-out told me I wasn't going to get it back, topped with the news that I was stupid to loan it to him in the first place.

That *dick*!

He was right. I should never have loaned it to him in the first place. But he taught me a lesson that cost me less than two dollars. I don't loan money no matter how much someone promises to pay it back. If someone I care about has a legitimate need and I am feeling generous, then I just give it to them. That way I'm not pissed when two years go by and I still haven't been paid back.

Remember, if they don't have the money now, they probably won't have an abundance of money anytime soon. It's okay to be generous, just don't expect to see the money again.

#48 YOU CAN'T BE ANYTHING WORTH BEING IF YOU DON'T KNOW ANYTHING WORTH KNOWING

When a chapter title is that long, there isn't much more for me to say.

But you know me. I'm gonna say it anyway.

Years ago, I hung a light fixture above my dining room table. Even though it works and has never started a fire, I know I'm never going to be anyone's first choice to do electrical work in their family home. I've never taken the time to learn more than the basics. I'm basically a *nobody* in the world of home lighting installation.

We all want to matter. The problem is, "mattering" is the hard part. It means we have to learn how to be a great parent, study for years to become a dentist or artist, or climb our way up to the top sales job. It's funny; so many times we want to matter, yet we don't want to put in the time it takes to make ourselves special.

We can learn a lot by watching TV. And nearly all of it is worthless. We can learn all the tricks to beat a video game, but when we turn off the console, we're not any better prepared for life than we were when we sat down. What can we learn that will add value to our lives and to our jobs? That is the question.

To be something we're proud of, we have to work at it. We have to put in the time to develop the expertise it takes to be successful. But the good news is, if you do it, you'll stand out in a crowd of people who *want* to matter but don't want to put in the time to learn *how* they can matter.

#49 AS SOON AS YOU HAVE A LITTLE MONEY, SOMEONE WILL BE HAPPY TO TAKE IT FROM YOU

My dad didn't have a lot of money, but when he died, he left all six of us kids an inheritance of about $20,000 each. One of my siblings was so happy to suddenly have a decent chunk of money that she bragged about it to the people at her work.

Big mistake.

Within a few days, a co-worker wrote her a heartfelt letter asking for money so he could enroll in law school. He even referred to her as "sister" in the Christian sense, appealing to her religious beliefs. My sister, having the kindest heart ever, gave this moron thousands of dollars and of course, she never got it back.

The letter this idiot wrote my sister had all the style and skill of a sixth-grade dropout. The worst law school in the country would never have accepted him. My sister should have spotted this red flag, but like I said, she wanted to do something nice for someone.

It's tempting to let people know when you have a little money in your pocket. It's hard to hide that you're doing pretty well if there's suddenly a Porsche parked in your driveway.

Just avoid advertising that your grandpa left you $42 million, or you'll be surrounded by people with their hands out.

#50 LIVE WITHIN YOUR MEANS

I'm going to jump to the conclusion that you floss regularly, pay your bills on time, and rarely speed drunkenly through school zones.

I'm also hoping that you resist the temptation to max out your Visa for that new TV with 3D Dolby Surround

Sound Featuring Mega-Bass Taint Massager.

I grew up without a lot of money, which has served me well. To me, a trip to the Black Hills is still, today, a kick-ass vacation. I don't need a $5,000-per-person Mediterranean cruise to feel like I made the most of my time off. I drive a ten-year-old car. Okay, I'll admit, it's a really *nice* ten-year-old car, but I don't feel the need to show off to my neighbors by getting a new model every three years. And let's face it: no one is ever really impressed with your car anyway, unless you are in high school and being judged by the quality of the stereo.

I know a lot of people who earn good money and should have enough to plop some into a 401k every month, but instead they are pretty much broke. They're late on their credit card payment, borrowing from their parents to make house payments, and are saying no to braces for their kids, but they have a shiny new Mustang, a new Jacuzzi on their new deck, and just got back from a week in Aruba.

I think the simple concept of "Never spend more than you earn" is an easy one to follow and I heartily recommend it. It's easier to sleep at night in a bed you already paid for, than to lay awake in worry on your diamond-encrusted deluxe Dream-O-Rama.

I'll throw in one more tip on avoiding a life of living paycheck to paycheck. *Don't have a kid if you can't afford to take care of it.*

"But wait!" people cry. "That's not fair! You're saying only rich people should have kids!"

No, I'm saying only *attractive* people should have kids. There are way too many ugly people out there.

Okay, but seriously.

Having a kid means expenses, such as diapers, day-care, and swings that hang from the doorway and bounce up and down. But wait, there's so much more. Every kid should grow up with more than just the bare minimums for survival. That means hockey equipment, Girl Scout uniforms, and a clarinet for band. If you can't give a child something more than the basics, put off becoming a parent until you can. Life will be a lot more enjoyable for both of you!

While we're on this, don't have a baby with someone who's shown no responsibility in their life. They will not be there for you financially or otherwise. You'll have at least eighteen years of hard work and expenses to face on your own if you make a baby with that person.

The fastest path to a life of never having enough money is to have a kid you can't afford to take care of.

It's the first toppling domino in a chain of being broke for life.

#51 LET'S BE HONEST ABOUT SEX

Sex can be awesome. It feels good and it's cheap entertainment. But just like smoking and overeating can feel great in the moment, sex is fraught with pitfalls. Danger lurks behind every corner. Listen up, because I've learned a lot about sex through trial and error, and no, I'm not talking about that whole "cutting a hole in a Nerf ball" incident.

Here's what I *think* I know about sex.

In general, women have sex for a relationship, either because they want one or they think they are in one. Guys have sex because it feels good. That's it. Are we that shallow? Sometimes, no; most of the time, yes.

"Don't go around breaking young girls' hearts. (*HE-HEEEE!*)"

Some people are forever fans of Michael Jackson, while others think he was one hundred miles of creepy. But no matter what you think of him, you have to admit, he *nailed it* in this line from "Billie Jean."

How does a guy usually break a young girl's heart? Most of the time, it's by dating her just for sex. See, guys will do just about anything for sex. They'll spend money, they'll listen to her talk all night, and they'll basically pretend they like her, all just to get in her pants. What happens when they get tired of sleeping with her? They dump her and leave her heartbroken.

I've mentioned earlier that women sometimes view sex as a sign the guy likes her. So they don't usually get in the sack until they really like the guy.

Guy meets girl. He wants sex. She wants a relationship. He pretends he does too. She has sex with him. He leaves. She's heartbroken. He then tells all his buddies what a psycho she is because she thought they had a relationship. She tells all her girlfriends what a jerk he is for sleeping with her and then dumping her. It is a pattern that has stood the test of time.

Is it going to change anytime soon? Probably not, but you should know how it tends to work so you don't get caught off guard.

#52 MEN ARE NOT AFRAID OF INDEPENDENT WOMEN

We hear it all the time. "Men are scared of me because I'm independent. That's why I'm still single!"

While there may be men who truly don't like independent women, these men aren't much of a catch, to be completely honest. All *good* men really *do* like a genuinely independent woman. They want a partner who has her own interests, can take care of herself, and has a life of her own.

But it seems like a lot of women who describe themselves as "independent" are really more self-centered than anything else. They're doing their own thing at the expense of being interested in their partner. That's not good.

Let's back up a second. What do we all love? We all love attention, right? We all love knowing that we're important to someone, that we matter to him or her, and that we make his or her life better.

Someone who considers herself an independent woman might, just *might,* instead, be so focused on her career, her yoga classes, and her trip to Vegas with the girls, that her boyfriend gets bored and walks away. He didn't feel needed or appreciated, so he went to look for it somewhere else. Most men *do* want a relationship, a partnership where they feel needed.

You've heard women complain about men who concentrate too much on work, their golf game, and their poker night. Yet these men aren't called independent; they're called selfish. Double standard? Independent women are great, but there's a fine line between *independent* and *self-absorbed.*

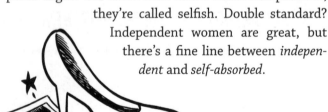

#53 THE WRONG PARTNER CAN SCREW UP YOUR WHOLE LIFE

There's an old episode of *The Twilight Zone* called "Spur of the Moment" where a woman is about to marry a boring guy and she's not super crazy about him. He's a good guy, but he just doesn't do it for her.

The night before her wedding, her old boyfriend comes by and she sneaks outside to see him. She's *crazy* about him. He's fun, he's sexy, and he wants her to run away with him. So she does.

Twenty years later, Mr. Fun & Sexy became Mr. Raging Drunk who blew all her family money. They lost their house, and as you may have guessed, they didn't hit it off very well anymore. She realized the hard way that she married the wrong guy.

I'm not saying she should have married the boring guy whom she didn't love, but I will say this: don't marry someone with a lot of drama. If you do, you will spend your life dealing with their drama instead of enjoying life. Maybe she loves the thrill of shoplifting or getting drunk or spending money she doesn't have. Or maybe he can't keep a job because the boss always has it out for him. After a while, you see the pattern.

If his favorite subject is himself, if he orders you around, or if he blames you for things that go wrong in his life, that's a bad sign. How can you go out with your friends, take a class, or go break a leg learning to snow-board if he requires constant attention from you?

The sexier, hotter, live-on-the-edge partner might seem like more fun, but when you've got a colicky baby on your lap and it's four o'clock in the morning, you're not going to want the partner who hasn't made it home from the casino yet.

#54 CONDOMS ARE TOTALLY WORTH IT

They say wearing a condom is like wearing a raincoat in the shower. It's like missing the ending of a great movie. It's like going to Hawaii and staying in your hotel room the whole time. It's also like having sex with a hunk of latex blocking all sensation. Besides, putting one on can be a mood killer. I get all of that, trust me.

But there are benefits to using these God-awful things. Topping the list of benefits is that you don't spend two weeks or more wondering if you're about to parent a child with someone you might not know or might not even like very much. Plus, you won't be worrying about burning urination and pesky sores. There's always that.

You can figure that any partner who doesn't want to use one has probably banged their entire block without using one, and you don't want any of that rubbin' all up on you.

You'll get to a point in a relationship where you probably won't need to use them anymore. But until you're that trusting, a condom is your best protection. A couple bucks and a fifteen-second pause in the passion is totally worth it.

#55 DONE MEANS *DONE*

The movies make us think that when someone says *no*, they mean *try harder*. In the movie, the guy shows up at the girl's work with flowers and wins her back in one short scene. That is not real life.

That is not real life.

A much more likely outcome is she'll get a restraining order to keep him away from her. When the cops arrive at his house or workplace to serve him, it is pretty embarrassing. Even more embarrassing is when he has to spend thirty days in the workhouse for not complying with the restraining order. Stuff like that is *super* difficult to explain to your boss.

"Uh, yeah, I'm going on a religious retreat and I won't be back for exactly one month. Hope that's not going to be a problem."

Good luck with that.

If the person you're dating tells you it's over, respect that and save some of your dignity. Chasing anyone that hard makes you about as desirable as a bulldog humping your leg.

#56 IF YOU WANT WONDERFUL, YOU HAVE TO *BE* WONDERFUL

Do you know the girl who says, "I want a guy who makes great money and who knows how to treat a woman. I'm tired of dating losers!"

Or do you know the guy who says, "I want a girl with boobs out to here who has a nice apartment and her own liquor store!"

What is the real problem with these people? The girl is a part-time nail tech with $35,000 in credit card debt and the guy is morbidly obese, rarely showers, and just got fired from Starbucks.

Everybody wants to find the perfect partner or spouse: attractive, smart, well-paid, funny, and freaky in the bedroom. Here's the honest truth: we usually get someone with qualities approximately equal to our own. The same way we can't pull our eight-year-old Ford Focus into the BMW dealership and expect to trade it for a new 5 Series, we can't get the ideal partner without resembling something desirable ourselves.

We have to be realistic. You might not get the guy with a vacation home in France, but you'll be pretty happy with the guy who can find France on a map. If you find the right partner for *you*, you stand a good chance at being pretty damn happy!

#57 FIND OUT HOW YOUR PARTNER FIGHTS

I'm sure there were times when my mom and dad wanted to murder each other, but I never knew about it. They either fought behind closed doors, slipped each other hateful notes, or argued telepathically. I just don't remember ever hearing them argue.

Most couples are different than my folks. They scream, throw things, and loudly accuse each other of being communist sympathizers. They get in each other's face and threaten each other with everything from severe head trauma to divorce, and you can hear them from down the block or through the wall.

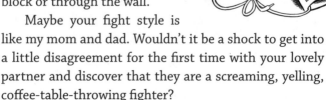

Maybe your fight style is like my mom and dad. Wouldn't it be a shock to get into a little disagreement for the first time with your lovely partner and discover that they are a screaming, yelling, coffee-table-throwing fighter?

It might not be a deal-breaker, but personally, I couldn't be with the latter. I just don't fight that way. It's not in me.

If you're in a relationship and you've never had a fight with him or her before, go pick one with them now and find out how they fight. I'll wait right here where it's safe.

#58 BEING MARRIED IS LIKE EATING CHEESE PIZZA EVERY NIGHT

Everybody knows this couple. She's gorgeous and he's sleeping with some troll who sanitizes shoes at the bowling alley. We wonder why in the world he'd ever cheat on such a beautiful woman, and with a woman like *her* no less!

Here's why: if this woman he's cheating on is beautiful, you have to figure he's got to be pretty attractive too. Attractive people attract other people, plain and simple. A lot of guys can't resist all this extra attention, so they cheat.

My wife is beautiful. When we were dating, guys would hit on her right in front of me. I swear I heard them whisper, "Why are you with this guy? Come home with *me*." Women will do the same thing, "Why are you with *her*? You need to take *me* out."

Why do men usually cheat with women who aren't nearly as attractive as their wives? I can explain in two words: cheese pizza.

See, when we first get together, we're always excited to have sex. It's like having a bacon cheeseburger supreme pizza with extra bacon, every single time.

After a while, sex is still good but not quite as exciting as it used to be. Now it feels more like having a cheese pizza. It's still pizza, and it ain't bad, but it's *cheese pizza*. That's when variety starts to look a little more enticing.

Have enough cheese pizza and you will crave something else, even something as God-awful as those mysterious beige things on the roller-grill down at the gas station. After years of the same cheese pizza, they start to look pretty tempting, even though they look and taste like the bottom of a shoe.

The girl at the bowling alley might not look like much, but she's *different*. I could conclude by telling you that you have to make sure your pizza never becomes a cheese pizza, but that would mean coming up with bedroom suggestions for you. And you don't want to hear my ideas on *that*, because my best bedroom tip involves a jar of peanut butter and a Duraflame log.

Is there any way to spot a partner who might cheat? Fortunately, yes. As cliché as it sounds, "Once a cheater, always a cheater" is a good gauge. Maybe they used to cheat, and swear they don't anymore. Great. Trust them. But watch for the red flags. I had a girlfriend who had cheated before but swore she wouldn't cheat on me. She would stop at a gas station on her way home from some guy's house and splash a little gas on her to cover the "man scent." When she got home reeking of gas, she'd say, "Oh, I'm so clumsy! I was getting gas and got it all over me!" After this had happened about five times, I started to catch on.

Stay away from the girl at the bowling alley. You'll feel way better about going home to cheese pizza. Maybe go online and order some, *ahem*... "pepperoni" and "black olives" to go with it.

#59 COOL AND THOUGHTFUL STUFF FOR YOUR PARTNER

Flowers and jewelry are great, but how about getting her car detailed instead? Especially if you've got little kids, her car is probably decorated with Goldfish cracker crumbs and smashed fruit snacks. You never know what kind of gunk your kids have ground into the carpet and seats. Make an appointment, borrow her car, wait the hour or so it takes to get it done, and surprise her.

It might not seem like the most romantic surprise ever, but she'll thank you for it.

#60 PICK, PICK, PICK

Years ago, I got a letter at the radio station from a woman who was having trouble finding a boyfriend. In the letter she said, "I'm not picky. I just want a man who loves horses, likes to run, wants a big family, and has no facial hair. Oh, and he needs to be at least six feet tall."

No wonder this woman was single! She had just ruled out about 98 percent of all the guys out there! What if

she met a great guy who was five feet, ten inches tall? Too bad, because she'd ruled him out before she even gave him a chance. Judging by the list of qualifications she wrote in her letter, I would venture to guess that she had other unspoken requirements as well. Unless she changed her mindset, this woman is probably still single today.

If this hits close to home for you, just remember there ain't *nobody* who is perfect.

#61 SMOKIN' THE WEED

I don't smoke weed. I think life is fun enough AND challenging enough without it.

I don't have a problem with people who smoke it, but I can honestly say that I've never once met a person who regularly smokes weed who is more than moderately ambitious. In my unscientific focus group of friends and acquaintances who partake, most are good people with jobs who pay taxes and buy Christmas wreaths from the Boy Scouts every year. But I can't think of any who would make me say, "Wow, that guy is really *going places*!"

The funny thing is, I don't blame their character. I blame them for choosing to smoke weed. I'm confident that if they put down the one-hitter five out of seven days a week, they'd be a lot more ambitious.

Sorry, but it's true. Some people might be offended by this, but you can't argue with it.

#62 YOU ACTUALLY DO LOOK YOUR AGE

If you think you look ten years younger than you are, you probably don't. Oh, I know people *tell* you that you do, but they don't mean it. Here's how you got the idea that you look ten years younger than you do:

You: It's my birthday today!

Them: Really? How old are you?

You: How old would you guess I am?

Here's where they pause and play this out in their head. *Okay, she looks like she's mid-forties, pushing fifty, but if I say forty-five, that won't flatter her. And besides, what if I say forty-five and she's only forty? That'll make her feel terrible! Better play it safe and guess thirty-five because there is no way in hell she's actually that young.*

THEM: I'd guess you're thirty-five!

YOU: OMG, that's so sweet! Would you believe I'm actually forty-five?

THEM: Shut the fuck up!

No, we don't look ten years younger than our actual age. We might look good for our age, but truth be told, we probably look our age. Oh, and while I'm being honest, no one thinks you are your daughter's sister either!

I know it sucks to get older. One day you're hanging with your twenty-two-year-old friends and the next

Don't pout about getting older.

thing you know, you're feeling out of place and saying, "Was I really that obnoxious and stupid when I was twenty-two?" (Yes, you were.) You're suddenly at an age where you feel slightly uncomfortable being at a bar with a bunch of college kids. That's okay, it happens to the best of us. Don't pout about getting older.

At thirty-nine, you might not make a great twenty-five-year-old anymore, but you can be *fantastic* at almost forty. If you're in your forties or fifties, don't dress or act like you did in your twenties. Remember, we can age gracefully.

#63 WHY YOU HATE GOING TO THE GYM

You know this story. You join a gym with big plans to get all healthy, toned up, and sexy. You pay the big fee and maybe even buy some new workout clothes.

And you go once.

It's the same with buying that treadmill or elliptical machine. Big hopes are dashed because you never use it.

I think I've figured out why this happens to all of us. Gyms are boring, treadmills are tedious, and ellipticals are mind-numbing machines of monotony. Even if you want to get fit or lose weight, you lose interest because you're BORED.

Yeah, I know. Some people love going to the gym and lifting weights. Some people love their treadmill. If you're one of *those* people, you can skip to the next story. Most of us want to have some kind of fun, rather than watch the miles *sloooooowly* tick by, while praying for our run to be over.

So how do you make working out fun? Don't work out. *Play.* Play basketball. Play tennis. Skate. Dance. Instead of running for fitness, run to get ready for your first 5K race.

I run. I hate the treadmill because it's boring, even with a television to watch. But I do it because it keeps me ready to run outside. Running outside is fun enough for me that I'm able to stick with it. If you want to stick with your fitness goals, find something fun to *play*.

#64 CIGARETTES ARE DELICIOUS, SMOKY GOODNESS

I had my first cigarette when I was in *kindergarten*.

At an age when most people are still occasionally wetting their pants, I had a Benson & Hedges 100 dangling out of my mouth. I didn't like it; I just smoked it because my best friend did.

But by the time I was twenty, I loved a good smoke. Soon after, I was solidly hooked. I'd smoke at my computer. I'd smoke while watching TV. I'd smoke in my car

There is no ONE cigarette that will finally satisfy your craving.

with my five-year-old daughter in the backseat asking, "Daddy, why do you always smoke?"

I quit once for a year. But then I had just one cigarette and the next thing I knew, I was at the gas station getting a savory pack of Marlboro Lights.

One day, a guy at the mall made me do a double take. He was in a wheelchair with an oxygen tank on his lap. His teenage daughter was pushing him around. Not fun for either of them, and it made me think long and hard about my habit. Would I want my daughter pushing my ass around while I wore some attractive, snotty, yellowing tubes in my nose?

What made me eventually quit for good was my parents. When I was fifteen, I promised my grandma that I'd never smoke in exchange for a hundred dollar bill. If Mom and Dad found out, I'd look like a total asshole. So, as an adult, when I'd visit them, I'd quit for the few days I was there. After one of my visits, I just never started smoking again.

Cigarettes are awesome. They're relaxing. They're satisfying. They give your lungs an invigorating little burn. And they're chemically addictive too, so yeah, there's that working against you.

Quitting isn't that hard. Just know this: there is no ONE cigarette that will finally satisfy your craving. You'll say, "Just one more" a thousand times. And ten months later, you'll want one again. Once I realized that, I stopped looking for the satisfaction in it all and quit smoking for good.

#65 DON'T TRY DRUGS

Not even once. Sure you've smoked pot. Almost everyone has tried it. I'm talking about the hard stuff. Why anyone would take a chance on that, seeing what it's done to other people's lives, is beyond my understanding.

There are countless "Don't try drugs" stories and here's another. A teenage boy had a sleepover when some friends came by. These friends brought along some heroin for everyone to try. All these athletic, intelligent, accomplished young boys gave in to the pressure to try it. One of the boys passed out. The rest of the boys hoped he would sleep it off and be fine in the morning.

The next morning, the boy was dead.

Here was a young kid who was loved by his parents, friends, and family, but for reasons none of them will ever understand, he made a horrible mistake. His parents will hurt forever, all because of drugs. He didn't try them to numb pain or cope with anything; he took them for *fun*.

Yes, life is hard sometimes, but the idea of taking the pain away with drugs is about as smart as putting out a fire by throwing gas on it.

You just can't try it. Nope, not even once.

Part 3

Don't
STEAL
anything

#66 DON'T STEAL ANYTHING

"Don't steal anything" is the third rule in my "Big Three." It's a rule we all know and most of us adhere to it. If you don't, stop it right now.

When I was nineteen years old, I overheard my boss scolding a kid at work who got busted for stealing Hall & Oates concert tickets. My boss hissed, "I hate a thief!"

I get it. Seeing Hall & Oates live in concert would totally kick ass, right? But a couple of concert tickets isn't worth your reputation. And as financially rewarding as it is to steal grandma's identity to buy sweet-ass rims, it still isn't worth it. It isn't worth it because you're stealing much more than money. And you're risking much more than "getting caught."

Some people steal all the time and think nothing of it. The thing about stealing is that it will follow you around forever. If people have an inkling that things disappear when you're around, then every time someone is missing their stapler, *you* get the blame for it.

"I'll bet Pete stole my stapler. He's the one who stole my burrito out of the fridge." They'll think it was you, Pete ... even if it wasn't you THIS time.

#67 GO RIGHT AHEAD AND BE JUDGMENTAL

The new mantra of our society is these three simple words:

"Don't judge me."

Or its close relative, "Who are you to judge me?"

Yes, you're right. You're unemployed, pregnant with your seventh baby, and spending your assistance money on wine. Nope, nothing that I should find wrong there!

The worst part is that people think they're being all Biblical when they tell you not to judge. After all, didn't Jesus say, "Judge not, lest ye be judged"?

Here's the Dave Ryan interpretation: "Hey you idiots, you can't be disgusted with this prostitute because you are a bunch of losers, too!" Jesus wasn't saying prostitution was okay. He was saying the drunken wife beaters in the crowd had no room to talk.

None of us is perfect, but that doesn't mean we shouldn't be judgmental. In fact, this might shock you,

Judging has a purpose,
so judge away!

but being judgmental is our responsibility! If we didn't look down on tax cheats, animal abusers, adulterers, and meth heads, we would be saying their behavior is just fine. Why shouldn't everyone do it?

If your daughter were dating a guy who just held up the local hardware store, I doubt the words, "Who am I to judge?" would escape your mouth. Judging has a purpose, so judge away!

And I think it's safe to say that the people complaining loudest are the ones with the most to be ashamed of.

#68 DON'T BE AFRAID OF A MICROPHONE

Since I'm on the radio, this is a pet peeve of mine. When artists win a Grammy, they come up on stage and make a speech into a microphone that is about a foot from their mouth and it sounds great. When you make a speech at next year's Tanning Salon Owners Convention, the microphone in the Sheraton ballroom is not going to be that sophisticated. You actually need to talk into it if you want to be heard past the first two rows.

And please don't be that person who says, "Oh, I just *hate* microphones. I'm not going to use it." Well, that

might be fine for you, but for everyone who's eight seconds away from officially giving up trying to hear you, it's kind of a pain in the butt.

#69 SHUT UP IN THE MOVIES

Seriously, why don't people understand the simple concept of being quiet so the rest of us can hear the movie? Do we come into their house and talk while they're trying to watch Netflix?

Don't toss your half-eaten pop-corn and empty Junior Mints box on the floor, either. I mean, yes, technically you can, because some kid comes through and picks it all up later. Really, nothing should feel natural about tossing your trash on the floor, not anywhere. Pick up your trash and throw it away.

And whatever you do, shut up during the movie!

#70 COURTESY FLUSH

I'll be flat-out honest and tell you I'd never even heard of the concept of a courtesy flush until I saw the first *Austin Powers* movie. Wow, a courtesy flush is a genius idea! If you're home alone, you don't need to, but at a friend's house, at the airport, or at work, flush the moment you're finished doing your business. The world will be a better place for your actions.

#71 STAY BUSY

Did you know the state symbol of Utah is a beehive? That's because the early founders of the state recognized the value of turning off the TV, getting up off the couch, and getting some work done. Since bees are known to be busy and productive creatures, it seemed like a natural state symbol. Say what you want about Mormons, but I give props to any group of people that walked from Missouri to Utah while pushing a wheelbarrow full of flour and babies.

Busy people tend to be productive and are able to have a job that lets them take care of themselves and their noisy kids. So put down this stupid book and go clean your microwave. It's *filthy*.

#72 DON'T WATCH OTHER PEOPLE LIVE THEIR LIVES

A lot of people pride themselves on how much they know about celebrities and showbiz. If you don't listen to my radio show, it might surprise you to know that I pride myself on how little I know about it all. Why? Because knowing a lot about celebrities would mean spending a ton of time on the couch watching them live out their lives. To me, that's just wrong on so many levels.

Shouldn't we be out living our own lives?

Think about it this way: take away the screen and it's like we're just sitting there motionless for hours at a stretch. Shouldn't we be out living our own lives? Rather than watching some rich idiots on reality television, maybe it's better we find our own reality and live in that.

Here's another way to look at it: How do you think your life would play out on a reality television show? If you've done nothing in the past year that anyone would ever watch on television, then you need to put down the remote, put on some shoes, and leave the house!

#73 WHILE THERE IS TIME . . .

This is the first line in an old song by Steve Winwood called "The Finer Things."

"While there is time, let's go out and feel everything."

I was twenty years old the first time I heard this line and even back then, it really struck me.

Winwood's point is that one day we won't have time for all the things we want to try. One day we'll be too old, too sick, or too dead to do all the things we can do today.

I've never forgotten this lyric since the day I first heard it. It's a huge reminder that our time is limited, our

health will take a huge dump on us, and yes, one day we'll be dead. What then?

Don't wait around. Go out and live and do all that crazy stuff you want to do. Get that degree. Visit that exotic country. Try that strange food. Learn to rumba ... while there is time.

#74 YOUR KID AND HIS FILTHY MOUTH

I love swearing and am proud to say I can make a street hooker cringe with endless streams of obscenities.

But I don't let my kids swear in front of adults. My kids know better. In fact, I've never heard any of my kids swear, other than my son say, "What the crap?" every so often to his buddies.

> ## Dumb behavior doesn't happen in a vacuum.

I ran into an old friend awhile back who invited me over to her house to meet her family. She had a son who was about fifteen who had absolutely no problem dropping the F-bomb and every other kind of bomb in front of me. I was disappointed in my friend and the kind of kid she was raising. A few years later, when this same friend's kid went to prison for setting fire to a day care center, it all made a little more sense. Dumb behavior doesn't happen in a vacuum.

#75 WHAT ABOUT THAT HAIR?

If I see a kid with dyed pink or blue hair under the age of eighteen, I don't blame the kid. I blame the parent for letting the kid look stupid. "But they want to find their identity!" says the parent.

I say, "Oh really? How about they find an identity they can't acquire in twenty minutes over their bathroom sink?" Maybe if they choose "straight-A student" or "great soccer player" as their identity, then they'd have something that would actually make them proud.

"But it's just hair!" whines the parent of the kid. "What's the big deal?" Well, it's ugly, for one. And two, if a parent is screwing up something as simple as their kid's hair, God only knows what else they're screwing up.

#76 DON'T LET YOUR KIDS SLEEP IN YOUR BED

Kids are awesome. We love them to death. We'll do just about anything to make them happy . . . or to make them shut up.

When a kid cries at night because he doesn't want to go to bed, it's a quick and easy fix to just let him sleep in bed with you, right? Why not? It's better than having a miserable night of crying!

Well, wrong. I know people who simply cannot get their kid to sleep in his own bed at the age of five or older because his parents let him sleep in their bed when he was little. They put the kid in his own bed and ten minutes later, he cries to get in bed with them. So rather than lose sleep, the parents give in, which only makes the whole thing harder to fix.

Don't give into the temptation. Both you and the kid will be better off.

#77 FORGET DOLPHINS; SWIM WITH YOUR *KIDS*

If you are a parent, you'll understand that I like to think of myself as a cool parent. When my daughter was thirteen, she wanted to learn how to snowboard, so we took lessons together. I *could* have stayed in the warm lodge, sipping a domestic bottled beer and reading *People*. Nope, I was out there with her, tumbling uncontrollably down the hill, muttering obscenities and getting big bruises. And we loved every minute of it. We still snowboard together today.

If the snowboarding example doesn't work for you, let's use swimming. Go to any public pool and you'll see moms and dads sitting poolside, nodding without looking up from their phone as their kids scream, "Lookit, Mommy! Lookit!"

When you go to the pool with your kids, get in and swim with them. When you go to the amusement park, go on rides with them. Your kids would much rather have great memories of playing Marco Polo and going on roller coasters together than the memory of being in the pool and yelling, "Mom, watch this!"

#78 BOYS PEE STANDING UP, GIRLS PEE SITTING DOWN

There are quite a few parents who actually make their boys sit down to pee. I know it's really popular to strip away our kid's gender identity and tell him that both sexes are the same and wonderful in every way, but this is one of the last things on earth that only men can do. We pride ourselves on it. We write our names in the snow. We attack that urinal mint with the fervor usually reserved for hand-to-hand combat.

We pee standing up and we like it that way. So your little guy might miss here and there. It's part of being a boy. Teach him to clean it up. That's also part of being a boy.

#79 PLAY CATCH WITH YOUR KIDS

It's a great skill. It's relaxing. It's exercise. It's good bonding time. It's also about the least expensive thing you can do together. Here's one more thing about playing catch I'd never thought of before: it's a lesson in patience and attitude.

I learned this from my son Chase. When I'd throw a baseball over his head, instead of trudging slowly back through the weeds to get it, he'd run. Maybe not a full-on gallop, but enough of a run to show that he was still having fun. He was also a good sport about me being a piss-poor baseball thrower.

I now run after balls that my boys throw, and I've taught my younger son to do the same.

#80 SPEND TIME WITH YOU KIDS, PERIOD

"To be in your children's memories tomorrow, you have to be in their lives today."

—Barbara Johnson

I feel bad for parents who avoid their kids. We all know the dad who doesn't have custody of his kids and basically ignores the fact that they exist. Sure, this gives him much more time to visit the local casino to see the Styx Reunion Tour, but he misses out on the whole experience of having a kid who adores him.

And let me tell you, there is nothing like sharing a mutual love with your kid. Getting an adult to love you is easy. All you need is good looks and money. But kids? They see through all that. They love you because you spend time with them and show them you care about them.

Years later when you're old and they're adults, they will remember that you took time for them. But you only get those short childhood years to show them, so if you blow that, you're pretty much screwed.

#81 HAVE YOUR KIDS CALL THEIR GRANDPARENTS

By nature, grandparents are old and will die sooner than most of us. Once they die, the chance of them creating memories with your kids drops considerably. It's up to you to make sure you create good grandparent memories for your kids.

If you live close to your mom and dad, that's great. That means your kids can see their grandparents often. If Grandma and Grandpa are retired and live in Florida, your kids might go a year or more without seeing them. You don't want your kids to think of their grandparents as strangers, so get some decent pictures of them and put them up in your kids' room. Have your kids call them at least once a month. Your kids will probably hate doing it, but that's too bad. It won't hurt them to spend a few minutes telling your mom or dad about the dance recital, the flute lesson, or how the dog was on top of the neighbor's dog trying to hug it.

It doesn't compare with grandparents who can come by every week, but at least your kid will recognize them the next time he sees them. Plus, if you keep your kids fairly close with your mom and dad, you'll also have a better chance of the kids being comfortable staying with them for a weekend so you can go to Vegas.

#82 TEACH YOUR KIDS TO HAVE A CONVERSATION

"How was school?"

"Good."

"What did you do today?"

"Nothing."

"Do you know I'm about to strangle you?"

"Okay."

This is your typical kid doing everything they can to avoid having a conversation with an adult. My kids were experts at this until one day, I had enough.

Kids who won't talk to adults are cute, until they're about nine.

I explained that "How was your day?" means that the adult is trying to start a conversation. Their one-word responses kill any chance of a meaningful banter. I've told my son that "Good" won't work as an answer when I ask him how his ski trip went, so he'd better start coming up with some details.

Why is this even important? Because somewhere down the road, no matter what our profession, we all need to learn to have a decent conversation. Ever talk to an adult who fires back one-word answers when you try to talk to them? It doesn't last long, does it? They're either rude or creepy or both. After a while, you decide they're not worth the trouble and you avoid talking to them.

Kids who won't talk to adults are cute, until they're about nine. After that, it's just weird and rude. I used to order for my kids at restaurants after they whispered to me "I want chicken strips." Not anymore. A server is a perfect, non-threatening person for a kid to practice on. Stop ordering for them.

#83 DON'T PUSH YOUR KIDS' SNOOZE ALARM

You're busy. I'm busy. Who has time to play Candyland with an annoying five-year-old? Well, no one. You've got work to do, you've got songs to download, and you haven't been to the gym in weeks.

So when your kid asks, "Mom, will you play Candyland with me?" you say something like "Just a second" or "Mommy's busy right now." That usually shuts your kid up for a few minutes.

Then sure enough, they're back at it, this time with dad. "Dad, can you play Candyland?"

"Nope, Daddy's setting up his online-dating profile right now." You're good for another ten minutes.

It's like our kids come with a tiny little snooze button, just like an alarm clock. The difference between your kid and your clock is that the goddamn clock never gives up on you. Ten minutes after you tell it no, the stupid thing is right back in your face.

Your kid is different. Your kid will eventually give up on you. She'll go find something to do without you, feeling rejected that you turned her down several times. She'll get the impression in her tiny little head that she isn't as important as the issue of *People* you're reading. She'll be less likely to ask next time, and worst of all, she'll have grown a tiny bit older.

"ONE DAY" BY DAVE RYAN

One day
Sooner than you think
The echoes of your child's laughter
Will have faded from your house

One day
Sooner than you think
Their bed will be empty
Their toys gone and their posters taken down

One day
Sooner than you think
Their messy room will be clean
And used for something else

One day
Sooner than you think
The house they lit up with their voices
Will be silent except for those soft noises adults
make

One day
Sooner than you think
Your kids will visit you
Just for a while when they have time

One day
Sooner than you think
The basketball hoop in the driveway
Will stand unused all year

One day
Sooner than you think
The swing set in the backyard
Will be given away

One day
Sooner than you think
Your child's spot at the dinner table
Will be empty

One day
Sooner than you think
Your house will be quiet
Between their visits

But today your child is home
And they want to spend time with you
Put off your work
And take that time

Because, one day...

#84 A PICTURE IS WORTH 442 WORDS

Wait, isn't it supposed to be a thousand words? Yeah, probably, but hear me out.

I have tons of pictures of each of my four kids. I have hundreds of hours of videos of plays, concerts, dance recitals, ball games, and rides on the teacups at Disneyland.

These pictures and videos reside happily in boxes buried beneath other boxes in the basement. Oh sure, I'm glad I have them, but did I really need *so many*?

Go to any kid's event and you will find a boatload of parents watching the entire thing through the lens of their cameras. They're making sure they get every second of little Joshie taking a fifty-dollar camel ride at the zoo on a video they'll probably never watch again.

Trust me. I've taken those videos too. I love my kids beyond compare, but there's no way I want to watch twenty minutes of them wobbling around on a camel, *ever*. Even when they've grown up and left for college, thirty seconds is more than enough to capture the moment.

Watch your kids with your own eyes.

I've learned it's much better to be there, live, soaking it all in. Watch your kids with your own eyes, not through a lens or the screen on your phone, and enjoy it as it happens. No video will ever be as powerful as you living the moment with your kid.

#85 STOP TALKING AND EAT YOUR LUNCH

If I've eaten half my sandwich and you are still holding your first forkful of salad while you're telling me about your wedding plans, then please shut up and eat. Let me talk for a few minutes to even it all out.

Obviously, this never occurs to some people. If you're the one with a half-eaten beef 'n' cheddar, put your food down and start talking. If you're the one not digging into your salad, take notice of the situation and stop talking. I know you're excited about your upcoming colonoscopy, but let me get a word in edgewise so that we both can finish our food!

#86 OTHER PEOPLE AREN'T WATCHING US AS MUCH AS WE THINK

Have you ever had an ugly giant pimple on your face—one that made you embarrassed to be seen in public?

You even mentioned to a friend, "God, I've got this ugly zit on my forehead and it's huge."

Your friend replies honestly, "Oh, I didn't even notice it."

It's amazing how much we worry about what other people are thinking about us. It's only natural, really, because we all want to be seen as attractive. I have realized that other people just aren't paying attention to us. Why? Because they're all too busy worrying about what other people think of *them*!

When you're twenty,
YOU CARE WHAT EVERYONE THINKS.

When you're forty,
YOU STOP CARING WHAT EVERYONE THINKS.

When you're sixty,
YOU REALIZE NO ONE WAS EVER
THINKING ABOUT YOU IN THE FIRST PLACE...

When my daughter was about fourteen, she couldn't even run to Target if her hair was out of place or if she was wearing a ratty shirt. I tried to tell her that no one was paying any attention, but she wasn't having it.

Not long ago, I was having lunch with an acquaintance who has a slight speech problem. Later, he told a mutual friend, "Dave must have thought I was an idiot because my speech was really bad when I was talking to him." Nope, not a chance. I didn't even notice because I was busy worrying about what he thought of *me*.

There is a great quote floating around from an unknown author: "When you're twenty, you care what everyone thinks. When you're forty, you stop caring what everyone thinks. When you're sixty, you realize no one was ever thinking about you in the first place."

#87 BULLIES ARE THE BIGGEST COWARDS

Just like you, I hate bullying. I hate bullies.

I wasn't picked on much in school, considering I was a kid with bad skin, terrible clothes, and a really bad, half-there mustache. But there was one kid in high school who was relentless.

"What happened to you? Looks like you got a bunch of snake bites on your face," was one of his favorites. And he always said it around an audience, because bullies are usually friendly when it's just the two of you.

One morning, as we waited for school to start, the bully sat down next to me and my group of friends. He looked at me and said, "Hey, it looks like you're growing strawberries on your face!" As clever as this line was, I'd had enough. Before I even thought about it, I punched him in the mouth.

Within seconds, blood poured from his lip. He rubbed his arm on his mouth and looked at the brilliant, crimson results. "Don't you know you're not supposed to hit a kid with braces?" said this loser who suddenly fell into the role of victim.

I sat there with my right fist still clenched, ready to deliver round two, and said, "You can only take so much shit!"

Bullies are cowards.

Bullies are cowards. I know kids are taught not to retaliate these days, but for this situation, it seemed to be what I needed to do.

The high-school bully never once bothered me again.

#88 HERE'S A CLUE TO SOMEONE'S *REAL* CHARACTER

An old dead guy named John Dalberg once said, "Absolute power corrupts absolutely."

I think what old-man Dalberg was saying is that *anyone* in a position where no one is allowed to challenge or question his power will always be an asshole.

Thankfully, we won't run into a lot of situations in our lives where we have to deal with someone who has absolute power. If you haven't already, you'll run into someone who abuses his or her power. Plenty of people in power will use it to line their pockets, take credit for the work of other people, scream at their employees, and be selfish in every possible way. They are missing the "I feel your pain" gene.

Most people who find themselves in a position of power will use it to accomplish their own agenda. Luckily, we live in a society where assholes aren't tolerated well. People end up calling them out on their selfishness. They usually disappear from the scene only to be a jerk somewhere else.

What about the people who don't have power themselves, but suck up to powerful people in order to get a little slice of power? I worked with someone years ago who shouldn't have had authority over anyone, but she did. She bullied and intimidated whoever got in her way. Even her own boss was afraid of her! Everyone saw it, but there wasn't a thing we could do about it.

Watch people in power. The lessons you learn will keep you from having to learn them the hard way. And remember, one day when YOU are in power, people will be watching.

#89 LET PEOPLE SAY NO

When I was in ninth grade, there was a kid in my science class named Mike Fabian. Believe it or not, his dad was an astronaut who went on to fly a couple of space shuttle missions. Mike was funny and he fit into pretty much the same junior-high social category as me: funny, somewhat dorky, invisible to girls, and a real smart-ass. We had a great time laughing it up in class and ogling girls we never had the nerve to talk to.

Several times I invited Mike to my house to hang out after school. He never even came close to accepting, but I didn't let up. If he said no one day, I'd just ask him again the next day, and the next day, and the next. I even found his number in the phone book once (remember when people did that?) and I called him. "Hey, you wanna come over and hang out?" His reasons for saying no were unclear. For all I knew, he had to be home to take care of his grandma, or he wanted nothing more than to watch reruns of *Andy Griffith*, or he needed to do homework.

Whatever his reasons were, I finally took the hint. Mike was a buddy at school but had no interest in hanging out at my house. It took me awhile, but I finally got it.

Isn't it annoying when you get invited to lunch with someone who's about as interesting as Chinese checkers, and you say, "Wow, I'd like to but I've got hemorrhoid surgery that day." So he suggests another day and you mumble something about how you're so busy teaching church youth group that you just can't find time.

"What about next month?" says the bore enthusiastically. This keeps up until you either give in or he finally understands. The next time you run into each other, you get the cold shoulder.

If you find yourself on the other side of this, stop pressuring a hesitant person. It's their loss if they don't want to hang out. Let them say no. They'll totally appreciate it.

#90 YOU CAN'T BUY FRIENDSHIP

It's hard to be taught a lesson like this when you're in first grade, but that's when I learned this one firsthand.

My big sister, Vivian, was driving me to school one day and we had to stop at the store for something. As I reached for a Hershey bar for me, I had a genius idea. I'd buy *two* Hershey's bars, one for me and one for the most popular kid in school, Mike Nasarellah, whom I wished could be my friend.

Mike was a badass. The first-grade girls wanted him. The first-grade boys wanted to *be* him. I decided I would be thrilled if I could buy his friendship with a candy bar.

At school, I proudly stuck out the slab of chocolate payola, smiled proudly, and said, "Mike, this is for you!"

Mike gladly took it and ate it with all the grace of a lion eating a zebra. *Cool!* I thought. *Mike is now my friend.*

It turns out he was my friend for a few days. I define the term "friend" loosely because Mike did not hang out with me. Hell, he didn't even speak to me. But I was still pretty sure that we were great friends!

About a week later, Mike was holding court as usual in the lunchroom where all the kids wrestled for seats close to "The Man." From his lunch-box, Mike produced a bag of Fritos. "Can I have some?" I said to my new friend.

"No!" he said as if I'd just asked for one of his kidneys.

Confused, I struggled to find the words. "But . . . but I gave you that candy bar the other day," reminding him of our special bond.

"Well," he replied, "you didn't *have* to." Then he turned to his audience of first-grade boys and continued being a badass.

That stuck with me. I'd like to say I never bothered with that worthless kid again, but I'm sure I still followed him around, trying to fit in with his circle of buddies. I learned that I couldn't buy someone's friendship. Mike taught me that some people won't like you even if you give them candy.

#91 SMALL TALK ISN'T SMALL

"So, how's the weather out your way?"

"Oh, it's gettin' warmer. We're probably going to have some flooding when spring comes."

"Yep. My brother's a farmer and he's pretty worried about flooding."

"Is that right? What does he grow?"

"Corn mostly. Some soybeans."

If this conversation wants to make you run a screw-driver through your eardrums, you aren't alone, but let's use it to rethink a few things.

Small talk is how we get to know each other. It's like a conversational handshake. Long before you realize you

Small talk is how we get to know each other.

both love Good Charlotte cover bands, you have to make small talk.

We all have said, "I hate small talk." Maybe you do, but like visiting your in-laws, you pretty much can't avoid it. The better you get at small talk, the better you will be at making meaningful connections, which will lead to opportunities and benefits you can't begin to imagine right now, like using their bass boat or staying at their cabin some weekend.

And isn't using other people what life is all about?

#92 THE EASIEST WAY TO MAKE CONVERSATION

You say you aren't good at making conversation? The good news is that you don't need an amazing set of skills to do this. The easiest way to make conversation is to ask the other person about their favorite subject.

Themselves.

Listen while they drone on and on and then ask them for some more. When you get bored, tell them how great it was talking to them and mention something about how you don't want to take up all their time. I'm not promoting shallow conversations, but making a point that making conversation isn't that hard. Try it and you'll see!

#93 SEND THANK-YOU NOTES

Thank-you notes are a dying tra-
dition in our society. Yes, you said
"thank you" when they bought your
newborn the obnoxiously loud Baby's
First Trumpet. You might have even
bragged on Facebook about that awesome baby shower your friends gave you.
None of that replaces a handwritten thank-you note.

Texting "Thanks for the live cobra! Little Bronx Mow-
gli really loves it!" isn't enough either. Be a grown-up.
Write a note, find a stamp, and mail the card.

#94 LET PEOPLE BE NICE TO YOU

We get a lot of snow in Minnesota. After a huge early spring snowstorm, our driveways were covered in more than a foot of heavy snow and everyone was armed with a shovel, heaving scoops of snow over their shoulders.

If you live anywhere that gets a lot of snow, you know what happens thirty seconds after you finally clear your driveway … *exactly*. The snowplow comes by and leaves a giant pile of crusty snow where the driveway meets the street. The neighbors are all back at it, shoveling the snow plow's "gift!"

This particular snowstorm, two young guys came out of nowhere, driving a truck with a plow on the front. They were going from driveway to driveway, clearing out the walls of snow left by the snowplow. Smiling from ear to ear, I gladly moved out of their way and watched them easily move the snowy menace onto my lawn. Amazingly, it only took them about thirty seconds to do it.

Instinctively, I fished in my pocket for a couple of bucks and walked up to the driver's window. He rolled it down, probably expecting a mere "thank you." I held the few dollars out to him and said, "Hey thanks! Here's a little something for your effort."

"Oh no," he said. "That's fine. You don't have to pay us for it."

But I wouldn't take no for an answer. "Nope, you take this," I demanded as I stuck the folded up bills in his shirt pocket.

I remember the look on his face. It wasn't one of gratitude. It was a mix of annoyance and embarrassment. He and his buddy weren't out to make money; they were just doing something *nice*.

We all like to be nice. We all like to help other people. We even feel satisfaction when we help strangers who can't thank us later. That's just the way we're made. We wouldn't think of doing our jobs for free just to be nice, but holding a door for someone, donating toys at Christmas, or helping some guy clear snow off his driveway *feels good*. It reminds us that we're good people, and in the process, we feel good for making someone else's life just a tiny bit easier. When I tried to pay the guys in the pickup truck, it cheapened their feeling of satisfaction, and that's not what they were looking for.

We all like to be nice.

Let people be nice without feeling like you owe them something. Lots of times, a genuine "thank you" is the greatest honor you could give them.

#95 APOLOGIZE ... JUST APOLOGIZE

I was in trouble for something at work. I was young and stupid and said something negative on the air about a restaurant that advertised on our station.

Advertisers don't like that. After all, they're paying big money to the radio station to improve their image. They generally don't appreciate some idiot deejay talking trash about them on the same station. I can't remember if I said their service was slow, the food was bad, or I'd spotted a dead body in their kitchen. Whatever it was, it got me a call from the boss.

My boss said something like, "You need to get on a call with Joe's House of Tripe. They're upset about what you said about a dead dog in the kitchen."

"I never said dead *dog*," I protested. "I'm pretty sure I said dead *body*."

"Well, whatever it was, they're pissed. Get in here now because we're going to have to call them!"

When advertisers get mad at radio stations, they often cancel their campaign. That means someone who worked hard at getting them to advertise with our station suddenly gets the account pulled out of their hands. It means the station makes less money, sometimes a *lot* less money. And sometimes that means people, idiots like me, lose their jobs. No matter what I had said, I didn't want any of that to happen. I knew I had to apologize in hopes that we could keep the account.

We get the owner of the restaurant on the phone and yep, he was more upset than I had imagined. "Why in the hell should I keep spending money on a station that's trashing my business?" The boss and I exchanged worried looks and I knew it was all on me.

"I can't tell you how sorry I am, sir. I made a stupid mistake and you have my sincere apologies. I completely regret saying you have dead bodies in your kitchen and it'll never happen again. I'm truly sorry."

Silence.

I was nervous.

Then more silence, followed by, "Well, uh, that's good. I'm glad to hear that. I enjoy working with your station and I'm happy that we can continue our relationship. Just be careful what you say from now on!"

In that moment, I learned about the power of a sincere apology. Instead of defending myself, saying it was just a light-hearted joke or that the restaurant really *is* a dump, I apologized. And it worked.

When you apologize to someone, the ball is in their court. Most of the time, a sincere apology works because the other person would sound like a complete idiot if they kept bitching at you after you apologize.

rly sry!

When you apologize to someone, the ball is in their court.

Most people won't keep pummeling you once you say you're sorry.

Remember, you can't simply *pretend* to be sorry. (I've tried that, too.) People see right through it.

Apologize, and mean it. It'll save your ass over and over and over again.

#96 WANT SOMEONE TO CHANGE?
JUST KEEP ON WAITING!

Lots of people call my radio show to vent about their boyfriend.

"He's gotten four DUIs this year, he dodges bill collectors, and he's running an illegal fur farm under our porch. But I'm staying with him because I'm sure he'll grow up as soon as our baby arrives!"

People change ... not a lot.

What?

Most of us have some experience with "The One Who Would Not Change." Either we were the one who waited for them to make a transformation, or we watched helplessly as our friend hoped his girlfriend would stop sleeping with the entire lacrosse team.

I dated a girl once who knew a guy who'd just gotten out of prison. Not jail, but actual prison. I can't remember what he got caught doing, but I think it was theft. For some forgotten reason, this guy wanted to borrow my kick-ass, expensive binoculars. Being overdue for another mistake in my life, I agreed.

Weeks later, when he still hadn't returned them, I naively asked my girlfriend to call him and have him bring them back. This is what he told her. "Yeah, I brought those by his house last week. When I looked in the window and saw him screwing some girl, I left."

Wow!

So, not only did I never see those binoculars again, but I also had to defend myself against this awesome and creative lie. Bonus! I guess I shouldn't have been so surprised that a career criminal would find it that easy to lie.

In the words of a former boss: "People change . . . not a lot." They may change a little or they may change for a short time. Oh, they'll *say* they will change because it'll buy them more time while you continue to pay their rent, but they will never *really* change.

There's only one occasion when you shouldn't give up on someone changing. Don't give up on your kid. You gotta keep on them so one day they can have a big house and you can live in *their* basement.

#97 TAKE THE COOKIE

We've all been there. A kid just made a batch of cookies.

"Wanna cookie?" your nephew asks as he thrusts a plate of shapeless lumps under your nose. "I made them myself!" he proclaims.

We all know that he probably didn't wash his hands before he started, and of course he licked the spoon halfway through and then stuck it back in the dough. You can't stop thinking about how the cookies look like a larger version of that thing that grew on your back last summer that your dermatologist had to biopsy.

Take the cookie. What kind of heartless bastard says no to an eight-year-old's homemade baked goods? He'll be so proud and happy that you took one. Chances are the cookie tastes better than it looks.

#98 STOP AT LEMONADE STANDS

I grew up out in the country where there was very little traffic, especially on our road. In fact, there was so little traffic that I had to put up my lemonade stand about a quarter mile from my house so I could be closer to the main road.

Only about one car came by every ten minutes, so sales were slower than at the Veggies 'N' Dip booth at the state fair. As ten-year-olds, my buddies and I were crushed. All the effort of our first business enterprise was going to waste. We were seconds away from deciding never to put effort in anything resembling work ever again, assuring our place in government dependence forever.

Then it happened. The man who delivered the paper saw us and bought a paper cup of our warm, watered-down swill. He gave us a dime and said those magical words: "Keep the change." How we ever expected to make any money selling Kool-Aid for a nickel shows what morons we were when it came to business.

But it made our day. Looking back, the man was not thirsty for a beverage some grubby little hands had prepared. He wanted to make us happy. I never forgot that. Next time you drive by a neighborhood kid selling lemonade, make sure you stop. Toss her a buck and tell her to "keep the change." It'll make her happy, and as a bonus, it might help her realize that work actually does pay off.

#99 GIFTS

I was about twenty-four and working at a radio station in Columbus, Ohio. One of our interns got me a Christmas present. Just by the package, I was pretty sure I knew what it was. I proclaimed, "I'll bet it's a coffee mug!"

Immediately, her face fell because it *was* a coffee mug. I'd ruined her surprise. That horrible feeling stuck with me. Now, someone could give me a packaged shaped exactly like a tennis racquet, and I'd completely play into the whole thing. I'd hold it to my ear, shake it, and ask the giver if it were a Velcro wallet.

Never make a genuine guess what a present might be as you're opening it. I know it's tempting and sometimes even easy to guess what's inside the package, but don't, because chances are, you might be right.

#100 DID YOU HEAR ABOUT LESTER AND PATRICE?

Yeah, they're sleeping together. They meet up in a parking lot out by the fairgrounds and have sex in her Expedition—the same Expedition her husband bought her.

Oh, this is getting good! And when you find out Lester's wife is pregnant with twins, it gets even juicier!

Most of us can't resist gossip. I don't blame you if you love it as much as I do. The only problem comes when you repeat what you just heard and eventually it works its way back to either the person you're gossiping about or the person who swore you to secrecy.

"Why did you tell Sheldon what I told you about Lester and Patrice? You can't keep a secret for shit!"

"Ummmmmmmm, well, uhhhhhhhh." You have nothing to say.

What's worse than gossip? Talking about someone behind their back is worse than gossip. What's the difference, you ask? Yes, there's a difference. Gossip is sharing juicy tidbits of information; talking behind someone's back is complaining about what a lazy, incompetent idiot they are and how they probably couldn't find their ass with both hands.

While everything you say may be true, the person you're bitching to is going to start thinking that you will talk about *them* behind *their* back, given the opportunity. It'll affect your friendship in ways you don't even know. The next time you are tempted to vent to a co-worker about how another co-worker is better qualified to be a hooker than a teacher, think before you speak.

Avoiding gossip is kind of like avoiding nachos. While nearly impossible, it's best to keep it in moderation.

#101 WHEN EVERYTHING'S OVER, HELP CLEAN UP

My dad lived to be eighty-eight years old. He was lucky to be in good shape for an old guy. He didn't like the thought of age slowing him down, so he resisted it. Maybe he wasn't doing the Ironman or playing rugby, but he did like to pitch in and help out whenever he could. He loved going to concerts once a month in his town's community center. When the concert was over, he always pitched in and helped put the chairs away. I can still picture my old man shuffling around with a metal folding chair under each arm. Meanwhile, all around him were young,

healthy people drinking coffee, chatting away, and barely noticing Dad's effort.

To some people, it just never occurs to them to pitch in. If you've ever had a kid in an organization like Cub Scouts or band boosters, you know that there are usually three people who do most of the work. The rest are happy to show up, eat the brownies you made, and chat while somebody else puts the chairs away.

I've got a rule with my kids: "Don't stand around and watch other people work." They hate it and that's how I know it's a good rule.

CONCLUSION

So there, you have it. All the shit I learned the hard way that now might help you.

If you read this entire book — you're awesome. If you didn't and skipped to the back, don't blame me when you get in trouble for getting your wife the same cheap flowers you got her last year (#59) or when your friend doesn't pay you back the ten grand you loaned her (#47).

In all seriousness, this book was a fun way to share the lessons that I've carried with me over the years. One final lesson before you go: Keep reading. Keep learning. Keep growing. Someone once told me, "As soon as you stop getting better, you start getting worse." As much as it sucks to think that we can't just "arrive" and be awesome forever, it's true. We have to keep getting better.

By the way, if you think you might want to share something YOU learned the hard way or even just say, "Hi!" you can email me at daveryanshowerbook@gmail.com.

If you just can't wait to hear more of my judgemental observations on life, check out my website at www.Dave RyanBook.com. That'll make at least one website your partner won't mind seeing while snooping through your browser history!

Pass this book along to someone you think might be able to use it. Or use it to prop up any wobbly furniture you may have.

Thanks for reading my book!

ACKNOWLEDGMENTS

I've been writing this book for years, but you wouldn't be holding it in your hands right now if it weren't for the encouragement of Dara Beevas from Wise Ink. Thanks to Heidi Sheard and Amy Quale for making it readable and for cleaning up my sometimes overly foul mouth. Big tip-o-the-lid to Kevin Cannon for his amazing artwork and to Ryan Scheife of Mayfly Design for designing the piece of literary magic you hold in your hands. Thanks to Steve "Steve-O" LaTart and Falen Bonsett for their patience and for "covering my shift" while I was writing. Most of all, thanks to my wife and family who for years, patiently tolerated me saying, "Not now, I'm working on my book!"

ABOUT THE AUTHOR

Dave Ryan grew up in Colorado Springs, Colorado, where he was a mediocre student, was chosen last in gym class, and never quite made Eagle Scout. Only upon discovering his love for radio did Dave make an effort at something for the first time in his life. Dave has worked in radio in his hometown, Las Vegas, Nevada; Columbus, Ohio; and Phoenix, Arizona, where he was fired twice in two years. He came to Minneapolis in 1993 to host the morning show on 101.3 KDWB. *The Dave Ryan Show* is now heard around the world on iHeartRadio and is one of the most recognized and respected in the radio industry. Dave is a pilot, a MENSA member, an avid motorcyclist, a snowboarder, and a four-time marathon finisher. He's also very judgmental, a chronic yo-yo dieter, and often spits when he talks. He has four kids and lives in Chanhassen, Minnesota, with his wife, his youngest son, and one too many pets.